PAT ROBERTSON

the
SHEPHERD
KING

The Life of David

ISBN 978-0-9986157-0-7

Today in the town of David a Savior has been
born to you; he is the Messiah, the Lord.

Luke 2:11

CONTENTS

PREFACE

A Portrait of a Unique Figure in Human History

David was a truly unique figure in human history. As we review his life, we think he exhibited a voracious appetite for romantic liaisons. He was a brilliant commander of his nation's armies. He was personally fearless and savagely brutal toward the enemies he encountered in battle. He was a brilliant administrator of the affairs of his nation. He became enormously wealthy in his lifetime. He was a gifted poet and musician.

In all of history, there have been few men who have exhibited such prophetic insight and overwhelming devotion to their Creator. He was the first in his lineage of kings and became the ancestor of the most important person who ever lived. Where else throughout history can such a man be found as the "Shepherd King"?

In the Bible there are seventy-five psalms which bear David's name, but the most famous of all of his psalms is Psalm 23. When David himself, a shepherd, actually viewed life through the lens of a sheep that was being led by Yahweh, the Great Shepherd, he concludes with these words: "Surely goodness and mercy will follow me all the days of my life and I will dwell in the house of Yahweh forever."

And so I begin this narrative with the words of the man who shepherded his nation for many years, "The LORD is my shepherd; I shall not want" (Psalm 23:1 NKJV).

CHAPTER ONE

A Handsome Young Shepherd Defends His Flock

Springtime in the Judean hills is beautiful. The air is filled with the scent of pine and cedar woods from the bountiful forests surrounding the hills. A canopy of lovely flowers adds its fragrance to the mix. It is a luxurious and beautiful setting. At night the stars shine with intensity and the grass in the pasture is lush and green.

In this setting, in the hills outside the town of Bethlehem, was a shepherd looking after a small flock of forty sheep belonging to his father, Jesse. These sheep were like family to him. He knew each one by its own name, and they came when he called and trusted him implicitly. This small flock of sheep comprised a significant part of Jesse's resources and, therefore, each sheep was precious.

Despite the beauty of the scene, the sheep became restless. Their terrified cries reached the ear of the shepherd, whose senses were immediately alerted to potential danger. He could make out the shape of an animal that was silently stalking his sheep. He crawled forward on his hands and knees until he was in a position to see the young lion silently approaching his flock. In an instant, the young shepherd leapt to his feet, ran forward, and threw himself on the back of the young lion. He locked his legs around the lion and then firmly grasped the head with both of his hands. With all his strength he twisted it, and the lion's neck was broken. The animal fell dead at the feet of the young shepherd.

This young man was named David, which can be translated into English as "beloved." He was the youngest son of his father, Jesse. He was smaller than his brothers and received his share of teasing from them. We cannot know whether they were actually jealous of his good looks or whether it was the natural order of big brothers to bully their younger siblings.

David was a remarkably handsome young man. We can imagine his appearance. His lips, unlike those of most older men, were full like a woman's. He was too young to have a beard, but his hair was flowing and golden. Despite the fact that he had been living outdoors for years, his face was not weather-beaten, but could be described as ruddy. Because of his constant physical exertion, his legs were strong and muscular, his chest was filled out, and his back rippled with muscles. He still had not attained his full height, but at fifteen, was about five feet, eight inches tall, and ultimately grew to a manly height of six feet.

During the Renaissance, the sculptor Michelangelo carved an idealized David out of Carrara marble, which reflected the artist's concept of how a fully grown David might appear. Located in Florence, Italy, this sculpture is considered one of the finest works ever created by the master. We can only imagine the real David would grow into such a figure as he later matured.

One of David's endearing attributes was his personal humility as well as his faith in God. He was incredibly handsome and a splendid specimen of a human being. But, fortunately, he was unaware of his own splendor. Unlike the man in Greek mythology named Narcissus, who one day gazed at a pool of water, saw his own reflection, and immediately fell in love with himself, David was never like that. Even though he was aware of his physical strength, his attention was not on himself, but on the majesty of the One who created the earth. David was never one to exalt himself, but in truth, viewed himself as a humble servant of God.

Of course, at age fifteen, the hormone testosterone was coursing through his body. The outlet for his adolescent urges became his vigorous outdoor life. But when he became older, those hormonal urges turned him toward the opposite sex, multiple marriages, and then a disastrous affair with Bathsheba, the wife of one of his trusted soldiers.

CHAPTER TWO

Middle-Aged Boaz Weds Gorgeous Ruth

This shepherd boy was descended from the tribe of Judah. In the early days, his ancestor Jacob had declared, "The scepter will not depart from Judah, nor the ruler's staff from between his feet, until he to whom it belongs shall come and the obedience of the nations shall be his" (Genesis 49:10). Young David knew nothing of this prophecy, but when he became king, first of Judah and then of all Israel, the prophecy was indeed fulfilled in him. One day he would be "the shepherd king."

David's ancestry is quite remarkable. His great-grandfather was Boaz and this is his story.

A famine had taken place in Israel. An Israelite man, Elimelek, and his wife, Naomi, had left Israel to go to Moab in search of food. They took with them their two sons, Mahlon and Kilion, and while in Moab, their sons married two Moabite women. Regrettably, both Elimelek and his two sons died in Moab, leaving their mother and two wives alone. The famine in Israel had abated, and the time seemed propitious for Naomi and her two daughters-in-law to return to Israel.

As Naomi started to leave, she told both Moabite daughters-in-law, Ruth and Orpah, that she would not be able to have more children to become husbands for them, recommending strongly that they return to their homeland in Moab and seek new marriages. After a tearful farewell, Orpah kissed Naomi goodbye and remained in Moab. However, Ruth made a memorable declaration. She said to Naomi, "Don't urge me to leave you or to turn back from you. Where you go I will go, and where you stay I will stay. Your people will be my people and your God my God" (Ruth 1:16). With that, Naomi and Ruth journeyed to the town of Bethlehem.

Hebrew Scripture offered a blessing for farmers in those days who would leave the corners of their fields unharvested so that the poor, especially widows and orphans, could eke out sustenance for themselves. Under Naomi's instructions, Ruth went out into the fields of a man of Bethlehem named Boaz to glean enough food for her and her mother-in-law.

She caught the eye of Boaz while she was gleaning his field, and he inquired of her, learning that she was the daughter-in-law of his relative, Naomi. So he instructed his workers to pay special attention to her, not to harm her, and ensure she was able to gain adequate food for her and Naomi. When Naomi received that report, she said to Ruth, "My daughter, I must find a home for you, where you will be well provided for. Now Boaz, with whose women you have worked, is a relative of ours. Tonight he will be winnowing barley on the threshing floor. Wash, put on perfume, and get dressed in your best clothes. Then go down to the threshing floor, but don't let him know you are there until he has finished eating and drinking. When he lies down, note the place where he is lying. Then go and uncover his feet and lie down. He will tell you what to do" (Ruth 3:1–4).

After a hard day's work and a modest supper, Boaz laid down to sleep on the threshing floor. You might wonder why a well-to-do farmer slept at such a place. Historic sources suggest that bandits were at large in the countryside, and a man like Boaz had to sleep where his grain had been harvested, lest thieves come in and steal it.

Ruth quietly approached the sleeping man, uncovered his feet, and laid down. When Boaz awoke, he saw in the dim light that a young woman had been sleeping at his feet. He instructed his workers to tell no one that she had been there. Ruth prepared to leave, but before she went, Boaz poured out a generous portion of grain for her to take with her. We are not totally certain what this action by an unwed woman meant, but it seems as if Ruth's actions indicated that she was available as a potential wife to this well-to-do man.

Boaz was a middle-aged man, and Ruth was a gorgeous young woman. He was enormously flattered by the fact that she would choose him over some of the handsome young men who were living in the area. Boaz went to Naomi and asked if she could enlighten him and whether Ruth would become his wife. Naomi told Boaz that there was a kinsman-redeemer, and that if he wanted to take Ruth in marriage, he would have to obtain the agreement of the kinsman-redeemer to stand aside. So, bursting with passion at the prospect of obtaining such a beautiful wife, Boaz lost no time in assembling the elders of the city to announce his intention.

When the elders of the city gathered, Boaz announced that he wished to purchase the land of his dead relative, Elimelek, but was forced to defer to the kinsman-redeemer who stood ahead of him in the family line. This gentleman immediately came forward and said, "I will redeem it" (Ruth 4:4). At which Boaz retorted, "On the day you buy the land from Naomi, you also acquire Ruth the Moabite, the dead man's widow, in order to maintain the name of the dead with his property" (Ruth 4:5). With that, the kinsman-redeemer said, "Then I cannot redeem it because I might endanger my own estate. You redeem it yourself. I cannot do it. ... Buy it yourself" (Ruth 4:6, 8). Then Boaz stepped forward and said to the assembled elders, "Today you are witnesses that I have bought from Naomi all the property of Elimelek, Kilion and Mahlon. I have also acquired Ruth the Moabite, Mahlon's widow, as my wife, in order to maintain the name of the dead with his property, so that his name will not disappear from among his family or from his hometown. Today you are witnesses!" (Ruth 4:9–10).

To seal the bargain, the kinsman-redeemer took off his sandal, and Boaz put it on. Then the council of elders crowded around him, shaking his hand, slapping him on the back, and wishing that he and his bride would have an abundance of children, would be blessed among the clans of Israel.

After marriage, Boaz slept with Ruth, who became pregnant, and she gave birth to a son. His name was Obed, and Obed in turn became the father of Jesse, who in turn became the father of David.

The ancestry of Boaz is fascinating as well. He is a direct descendant of a woman named Rahab. But who is Rahab?

When the Israelites under Joshua were preparing to attack the city of Jericho, two spies found refuge in the home of a woman named Rahab. Most biblical sources refer to Rahab as a prostitute. She was the owner of a large house and either she was a madam with a stable of prostitutes or, as some suggest, she was an innkeeper, not a prostitute. Whatever her profession, she hid the spies and exacted from them a promise that she and her family would be spared when Israel began the destruction of the city of Jericho. The spies told her to put a red thread outside of her house to identify it and to gather her family and to stay within the house during the upcoming battle. Their pledge would stand if she followed their directions; if not, they would not be bound. The spies slipped out under cover of darkness and reported to Joshua that the city of Jericho would be theirs.

True to their word, the Israelites spared Rahab and her family, and she in turn became the direct ancestor of Boaz, Obed, Jesse, and David.

David is the ancestor of Jesus Christ, and his ancestry was not merely Abraham, Isaac, and Jacob, but includes a Moabite who was one of Lot's descendants, and also a woman of Jericho who was clearly a Gentile. This, in turn, means that Jesus Christ was a representative not of merely one family, but of the entire human race.

CHAPTER THREE

A Wellspring of Praise

Out under the stars in the stillness of the night, David focused his attention on the majesty of the Creator. Deep within his heart there was a wellspring of praise and adoration to God which remains unsurpassed even to this day. Consider this exclamation of adoration for God when he wrote these words, "Lord, our Lord, how majestic is your name in all the earth! You have set your glory in the heavens. Through the praise of children and infants you have established a stronghold against your enemies, to silence the foe and the avenger. When I consider your heavens, the work of your fingers, the moon and the stars, which you have set in place, what is mankind that you are mindful of them, human beings that you care for them? You have made them a little lower than the angels and crowned them with glory and honor" (Psalm 8:1–5).

Alone in the Judean hills, David began to sing these songs; he played the harp beautifully, and his voice soon became a rich baritone. His beautiful music not only brought comfort and assurance to his little flock—but would also soothe the troubled heart of a king who slowly was descending into madness.

CHAPTER FOUR

Midianite Women Seduce God's People—
Levi's Priesthood Confirmed

When the children of Israel came out of Egypt, they were organized according to tribes and family units. Their leader was a monumental figure named Moses who received his direction directly from God Himself. The ordering of the lives of the people was given to Moses by God to be promulgated for the governing of the people. Specific laws, regulations, and commandments were clearly spelled out by God to Moses. God gave to Moses one set of regulations including commandments written by His hand on tablets that contained what are known as "The Ten Commandments." The Bible book known as Deuteronomy is taken from two words, *deuteros* and *nomas*, which together mean "second law." New regulations and broad sweeping principles for human conduct were laid out directly by God through His servant Moses. He promised Moses that as the children of Israel moved in their journeys, He would go before them and mark out the path that they should follow. God even provided direction for them in the form of a cloud by day and a pillar of fire by night. When the cloud rested, they were to stay still and rest. When the cloud lifted, they were to begin to move. As a people, they were successful because God Almighty was their ruler and, by His infinite knowledge, could care for each of them in ways they could not possibly do for themselves.

God spoke to Moses' successor, Joshua, before he began the conquest of Palestine. Joshua was told clearly, "Be strong and very courageous. Be careful to obey all the law my servant Moses gave you; do not turn from it to the right or to the left, that you may be successful wherever you go. Keep this Book of the Law always on your lips; meditate on it day and night, so that you may be careful to do everything written in it. Then you will be prosperous and successful. Have I not commanded you? Be strong and courageous. Do not be afraid; do not be discouraged, for the LORD your God will be with you wherever you go" (Joshua 1:7–9).

After the people were settled in the land, God placed over them a priest who was a member of the family of Abraham's great-grandson Levi. During times of crisis when Israel was ruled by enemies, God gave them a number of powerful leaders who provided critical leadership for a short period of time. Before the time of the kings, the reigning High Priest was a Levite named Eli. By law, Eli and his family had been generously provided for out of a portion of the offerings which the Israelite people brought to the temple. Regrettably, Eli became too old to exercise the authority that had been given to him. His full-grown sons took advantage of their failing old father and had become thoroughly reprobate. They stole the offerings that the people were bringing to the Lord. Not only did they commit this sin, but they actually forced sexual relations upon the dedicated women worshipers who had come to the temple to worship God. Eli warned them that this conduct would bring disaster upon the family, but they refused to listen to the old man who, by this time, had become very fat and was almost blind.

At that time, a man was living in Israel named Elkanah, who became the father of the prophet Samuel. As we search the ancestral records, we learn that Elkanah was actually a descendant of Jacob's son Levi. Levi had been given the task of caring for the sacred articles of the tabernacle and its furnishings as the children of Israel journeyed from Egypt to the Promised Land. We should remember that Moses and his brother, Aaron, were descendants from Amram and Jochebed, who themselves were part of the tribe of Levi, the spiritual leaders of Israel.

Although this story is well known, it bears repeating…

As hundreds of thousands of the Israelites moved steadily northward, a Canaanite king named Balak realized that he lacked even a fraction of the military strength needed to oppose this oncoming horde of people. So, he decided to try magic curses against them instead. King Balak sent representatives to the home of Balaam, a prophet conjuror. Balaam initially refused to go, but finally agreed to accompany Balak's representatives when they upped the offer for his services to a staggering amount.

As the story unfolded, Balaam was unable, under the power of God's Spirit, to utter any curse against the people of Israel. Finally, he stopped trying to curse them and instead brought forth a memorable benediction over them. It became obvious to Balak that the children of Israel would prevail over him unless their God lifted His mantle of protection.

But how was this to be accomplished? By the simple trick that has destroyed thousands of men during history—the seductive allure of promiscuous women.

Into the Israel camp trooped a bevy of young Midianite women. Astoundingly, they began to have sexual relations with the Israelite men in broad daylight and in the presence of Moses. They not only seduced the men sexually, they talked them into worshiping Baal Peor, and in so doing brought the wrath of God upon the people.

God spoke to Moses and told him to kill all of the leaders of the people who had allowed these terrible things to take place. While this was happening, an Israelite man brought into his tent a Midianite woman whose name was Cozbi, the daughter of Zur. This couple was engaging in sexual relations before Moses and all the people—in broad daylight. Then Phinehas, the grandson of Aaron, left the assembly and took a spear and thrust it through the back of the Israelite man and into the stomach of Cozbi, killing them both.

By this action, the plague against the people was stopped, but not until 24,000 of the Israelites had been killed. The action of Phinehas was so pleasing to the Lord that He told Moses, "Tell him I am making my covenant of peace with him. He and his descendants will have a covenant of a lasting priesthood, because he was zealous for the honor of his God and made atonement for the Israelites" (Numbers 25:12–13).

Hundreds of years later, we read in the Book of Malachi (2:4–7) the importance of Levi, where we are told:

> "'And you will know that I have sent you this warning so that my covenant with Levi may continue,' says the Lord Almighty. 'My covenant was with him, a covenant of life and peace, and I gave them to him; this called for reverence and he revered me and stood in awe of my name. True instruction was in his mouth and nothing false was found on his lips. He walked with me in peace and uprightness, and turned many from sin. 'For the lips of a priest ought to preserve knowledge, because he is the messenger of the Lord Almighty and people seek instruction from his mouth.'"*

(*This particular verse became the theme of a portion of *The 700 Club* television program—"Your Questions, Honest Answers.")

Now we return to the story of Samuel, a descendant of Levi and son of Hannah, who was a spiritual leader for many years over the entire nation of Israel…

Elkanah had two wives, Hannah and Peninnah. Peninnah had children and took delight in taunting Hannah who was unable to bear children. Hannah was miserable and, despite her husband's love and clear favoritism for her, she would not rest content until she got pregnant and had a baby.

Each year the family came to the tabernacle to bring offerings and to pray. During one such visit, Hannah was overcome with emotion and began to cry out to God with all her heart. She vowed to the Lord that if He would give her a son, she would dedicate him to the Lord's service to show her appreciation for His kindness. Eli observed her and thought she was drunk, so he rebuked her harshly and said, "How long are you going to stay drunk? Put away your wine" (1 Samuel 1:14). With tears running down her cheeks, Hannah said, "Not so, my lord. … I am a woman who is deeply troubled. I have not been drinking wine or beer; I was pouring out my soul to the Lord. Do not take your servant for a wicked woman; I have been praying here out of my great anguish and grief" (1 Samuel 1:15–16). At that, Eli replied, "Go in peace, and may the God of Israel grant you what you have asked of him" (1 Samuel 1:17).

The family returned home, Elkanah slept with Hannah, and, as she had prayed, she became pregnant. Nine months later she gave birth to a son, whom she called Samuel. True to her word, as soon as the little fellow was weaned, she took him back up to the tabernacle and said to Eli, "Pardon me, my lord. As surely as you live, I am the woman who stood here beside you praying to the Lord. I prayed for this child, and the Lord has granted me what I asked of him. So now I give him to the Lord. For his whole life he will be given over to the Lord" (1 Samuel 1:26–28).

Samuel lived in the tabernacle from then on, subject to Eli, and his duties included opening the tabernacle each day to allow worshipers to come in. We are told in 1 Samuel 3:7 that, as a young man, Samuel had never heard the voice of the Lord, but one night while he was asleep God spoke to him and said, "Samuel!" He thought he was being summoned by Eli, so he jumped up and ran to Eli, and said, "I am here. You called."

And Eli said, "I didn't call you. Go back to bed." So Samuel went back and laid down, and God called him again, "Samuel!" He jumped up and went back to Eli and said, "You called me."

The old priest said, "I didn't call you. Go back to bed."

This happened a third time, and Eli realized the voice of God was calling the young man. He told Samuel, "When He calls again, say, 'Speak, Lord. Your servant hears You,'" because he realized the voice of God was calling the young man.

So when God called him next, he said, "Speak, Lord. Your servant hears." And God said, "I'm going to do something that makes the ears of those who hear tingle. I have rejected Eli from the priesthood because he refuses to discipline his sons and they have become a disgrace throughout Israel."

The record is not clear on what went through Samuel's mind, but we can only imagine that, as a youngster, he had come to regard Eli as his father. In his respect for the old man, he was much too young to realize how remarkably outrageous Eli's older sons had become.

The next morning, Eli called Samuel to him and asked, "What did God tell you? Don't withhold one word from me."

Then Samuel reluctantly blurted out to him, "God said that He is going to remove you and your sons from the priesthood, and you will no longer enjoy the privileges you now have."

Eli replied, "He is the Lord. Let Him do what seems good."

The revelation of God to Samuel and Eli took place in secret, but God's plan was soon worked out on the battlefield. During all this time, the Philistine armies had been fighting the armies of Israel. In the initial skirmish, the Philistines won a fearsome battle. Then the Israelite troops told their commander, "We must have help from the Lord. Have them bring the Ark of the Covenant up to the battlefield along with the priests who can lead us in prayer."

So, two of the sons of Eli, Hophni and Phinehas, carried the Ark up to the battlefield, and when it appeared, the troops of Israel began to shout because they knew with God's help, they would be victorious. When the Philistines heard the noise, they were frightened because they remembered how the God of Israel had overcome the forces of Pharaoh of Egypt, and it was easy for them to believe that with God on the side of Israel, the Philistine cause was lost.

Nevertheless, the Commander of the Philistine army said, "Be strong, Philistines! Be men, or you will be subject to the Hebrews, as they have been to you. Be men, and fight!" (1 Samuel 4:9). In the next day's battle, the Philistines rallied and slaughtered the troops of Israel, killed both sons of Eli, and took the Ark of the Covenant captive. When Eli heard the word, he was stunned with fright, fell off the place where he had been sitting, and, because he was very fat, broke his neck and died. Then the Lord pronounced judgement upon Eli's sons and future descendants because of the evil things Eli had permitted to be done.

With Eli and his sons dead, we must presume that Samuel was left in charge of the tabernacle. As he grew older, God was clearly with him, and we are told that he "continued to grow in stature and in favor with the LORD and with people" (1 Samuel 2:26). By the time he was twenty years old, it became apparent that Samuel had become the spiritual leader of Israel and, as God's regent, was in charge of the country.

As often happens with great spiritual leaders, their offspring are not able to continue with the same fervor and integrity as their parents. This was true of Samuel's sons. As a result, the people of Israel began looking around for the next leader. They had failed to see they had been wonderfully blessed with God Himself and His prophets leading their nation. But now to their shame, they had begun looking at their neighbors who were led by kings. In village upon village all over Israel, groups began murmuring, "Why can't we have a king to lead our armies in battle like the other nations that surround us?" The murmuring became a loud chorus until it became a demand to Samuel that he appoint a king to rule over Israel.

Samuel, in his wisdom, warned them what it would mean. The king would take the best of their produce. He would exact taxes upon them. He would take their young men and women to become his household servants. He would draft their able-bodied men into his armies. Whereas they had enjoyed freedom under God for centuries, they were now going to exchange this freedom for the domination of a king.

When Samuel talked to the Lord about it, he was told, "Listen to all that the people are saying to you; it is not you they have rejected, but they have rejected me" (1 Samuel 8:7). So, He instructed Samuel to give the people what they requested.

This is the story of the future king… A man from Kish had lost some donkeys. He sent his son, Saul, to look for them, but he was unsuccessful. In those days, the prophet was called a *seer*. Saul believed that such a person could help him find the lost donkeys. So, he inquired around to find out where the seer lived.

As Saul was making his way toward Samuel's residence, God spoke to Samuel to tell him that he was sending the future king to him that day. You can only imagine how surprised Saul was when he met the seer and was invited to his home for a meal. Samuel continued, "As for the donkeys you lost three days ago, do not worry about them; they have been found. And to whom is all the desire of Israel turned, if not to you and your whole family line?" (1 Samuel 9:20).

When they entered the dining hall, Samuel instructed the cook, "Bring the piece of meat I gave you, the one I told you to lay aside" (1 Samuel 9:23). And Samuel said to Saul, "Here is what has been kept for you … because it was set aside for you for this occasion" (1 Samuel 9:24). After the meal was over and the guests had departed, Samuel approached Saul. Then he took a flask of oil and poured it on Saul's head. He told Saul precisely the things that would happen to him during the next few days, including that he would be filled with the Holy Spirit and would become a different person.

A few weeks later, Samuel called together the leaders of the clans of Israel to tell them that Saul, the son of Kish of the tribe of Benjamin, had been chosen by God as their next king. We are told that Saul was head and shoulders taller than his contemporaries, yet at the ceremony which marked his introduction to the elders of Israel, he hid in the baggage because he was too embarrassed by the honor bestowed upon him. Nevertheless, he was finally brought before the people. Samuel introduced him to the elders and said, "Here is your new king." And now this inexperienced and somewhat bashful young man became the king over God's people.

At this point, we see a serious flaw in Saul's makeup, which one day led to madness and destruction. Saul never fully believed that he was entitled to be king. He never believed that the kingship was secure in his hands—even though God had given it to him. He was unwilling to exercise the authority that had been given him and, therefore, was led into disobedience by his army commanders. It's amazing how a small lack of confidence in a young leader can ripen into a situation of national chaos at a future time. In truth, if a leader is not convinced of the legitimacy of his office or of his own power in that office, he can make a series of tragic blunders which will not only tear his country apart but will lead to his own destruction.

CHAPTER FIVE

An Emotionally Damaged Man Becomes King

Despite his limitations, Saul as king was able to mobilize enough of the Israelite people to defend a beleaguered tribe. From time to time, Saul performed skillfully as a military commander. He was undefeated in battle. Now as reigning king and successful military commander, it was natural for the prophet Samuel to come to him with a special instruction from God Almighty. Samuel said, "I am the one the LORD sent to anoint you king over his people Israel; so listen now to the message from the LORD. This is what the LORD Almighty says: 'I will punish the Amalekites for what they did to Israel when they waylaid them as they came up from Egypt. Now go, attack the Amalekites and totally destroy all that belongs to them. Do not spare them; put to death men and women, children and infants, cattle and sheep, camels and donkeys'" (1 Samuel 15:1–3). In obedience to these instructions, Saul mobilized his army and began a march against the Amalekites. On day one, they ruthlessly slaughtered those whom they had been instructed to slaughter. But, Saul and his commanders spared the beautiful cattle, healthy sheep and lambs. They even took Agag, king of the Amalekites, prisoner rather than killing him.

Hidden psychological and emotional deficiencies will come out in times of crisis. This was Saul's time of crisis and he failed—to his destruction. He could have done exactly what God told him to do, but instead he listened to the voice of his commanders and likely his own greed as the prospect of personal plunder took center stage in his life.

When Samuel met Saul again, Saul was wreathed in smiles and said, "The LORD bless you! I have carried out the LORD's instructions. Samuel replied, "What then is this bleating of sheep in my ears? What is this lowing of cattle that I hear?" (1 Samuel 15:13–14). And Saul said, "The soldiers took sheep and cattle from the plunder, the best of what was devoted to God, in order to sacrifice them to the LORD your God at Gilgal." To which, Samuel replied, "Does the LORD delight in burnt offerings and sacrifices as much as in obeying the voice of the LORD? To obey is better than sacrifice, and to heed is better than the fat of rams. For rebellion is like the sin of divination, and arrogance like the evil of idolatry. Because you have rejected the word of the LORD, he has rejected you as king" (1 Samuel 15:21–23).

Then King Agag came up thinking, "Surely the pain of death is over," but Samuel said, "As your sword has made women childless, so will your mother be childless among women," at which time he took the sword and hacked Agag to pieces (1 Samuel 15:33).

Saul said to Samuel, "I have sinned in failing to carry out God's instructions, but come and honor me before the people and let us offer a sacrifice together." Samuel accompanied Saul on this last mission, but after that had no further dealing with him until he spoke to him from the grave. God spoke to Samuel, "It grieves Me that I have made Saul king over Israel. He failed to carry out my instructions." Samuel did grieve over the failure of Saul and the collapse of his authority. Then the Lord spoke to him these words, "How long will you mourn for Saul, since I have rejected him as king over Israel? Fill your horn with oil and be on your way" (1 Samuel 16:1). The Lord had chosen another.

CHAPTER SIX

A Brave Teenager Brings Down a Giant

The pages of Israel's history under King Saul are filled with the suffering of the Israelite people from a group known as the Philistines. In what later became known as genocide, the Philistines oppressed the Israelites, stripping them of their weapons of war, and preventing them from prospering in their land. It was a relentless campaign of harassment, humiliation, and suffering. In struggle after struggle, we read of the cruelty of the Philistines.

However, one instance stands out in this particular narrative. King Saul was able to gather together a modest force of warriors in what is called the Valley of Elah. The Philistines were on one side of the valley, the Israelites on the other. Out of the Philistine ranks strode a giant whose name was Goliath. Goliath was over nine feet tall and had a bronze coat of armor that weighed about 125 pounds. His spear was like a weaver's rod and it weighed about fifteen pounds. He strode across the battlefield and shouted at the Israelites, "I challenge you to set a man against me. If he can beat me, we will be your servants. If I beat him, you will be my servants. Send me the champion!" Of course, the Israelites were terrified and no one in their ranks was capable of taking on this challenge.

About this time, the shepherd David was sent by his father to bring some bread and cheese for the troops. When he reached the front line, his older brother Eliab looked down at him and snarled, "Why aren't you looking after the sheep? You are just up here to watch the big show. Why don't you go home?"

But David inquired around to other men to find out what was the furor in the Valley of Elah. He was told that if anyone could beat Goliath, his family would be free from taxes and he would be given one of the king's daughters as his wife. David inquired of a second person and learned the same thing. So he wondered out loud, "Who is this uncircumcised Philistine that he would dare oppose the armies of the living God?"

David told the Israelite commander, "I will go up against the giant." When Saul heard of it, he said to David, "You are nothing but a youngster and Goliath is a hardened warrior. However, I will give you my armor so that you can fight him." David was then equipped with Saul's armor and, after it was on him, he found that he could hardly move. He reminded the king that he had killed a lion and he had killed a bear and he knew how to fight, but not with heavy armor on his body. So he stood without armor before the giant on the other side of the valley of Elah. Goliath looked at him and fumed, "Am I a dog that you would send a child to fight me?" And David yelled back, "You have defied the armies of the living God, and I will kill you and cut off your head."

Imagine what was going through David's mind at this time. He was only fifteen years old, yet he was making a bold stand in front of the entire army of Israel, not to mention his older brothers and the armies of the Philistines. If he failed, he would be dead and his entire family would be humiliated. He must have considered the difficulty for them in living down a failure of this magnitude in the days to come. Assuming he was successful, how difficult to face the jealousy of the entire Israelite army when he, a mere youngster, showed them to be weak cowards in front of a Philistine giant. Whether these thoughts actually went through his mind, we don't know. They certainly would occur to any modern-day teenager, but David was so full of God's power that these thoughts may never have crossed his mind. The thing that is certain is this—he had seen God work in his victory over a lion and a bear, and he knew the same God who had helped him in these encounters could also help him with a Philistine giant.

So David raced forward, selected several smooth stones the size of modern baseballs, and placed one of them in his sling. He ran close to Goliath, swung the sling around his head, and launched the missile straight and true. He hit Goliath with massive force right in his forehead. The giant fell forward unconscious. David rushed forward, grasped the giant's sword, and cut off his head, holding the bloody head up for all the soldiers to see as he shouted in triumph. At this, the Philistines fled in terror, and the Israelites won the day.

CHAPTER SEVEN

King Saul Descends into Madness

True to his word, Saul took David into his household and made him a member of his staff. David proved to be a skillful troop commander, and wherever he went his forces won battles.

Not long after, the young girls in Israel began to sing songs of joy as they danced alongside the returning troops. "Saul has killed his thousands," they sang, "and David has killed his tens of thousands." When these words came to Saul's ears, his deep-seated psychological insecurity came to the fore. He thought, "If this is what they are saying about David and me, it won't be long before they will want to take the kingship away from me."

The man who started his career hiding in the baggage compartment, who had never been secure in his own legitimacy, now began to lapse into a deep state of paranoia. Instead of rejoicing that his young commander was winning battles for him against the enemies of his nation, Saul sought to kill him as a potential rival to the throne. Day by day, this obsession grew within him until he no longer thought of governing the people of Israel. His mind was focused on ways that he could kill David.

Saul had promised that the man who killed Goliath would become his son-in-law, but despite the promise, he gave his oldest daughter in marriage to one of his officials. However, his younger daughter, Michal, loved David and wanted to marry him. So Saul now saw a chance to have his rival killed and instructed his officials to tell David, "The king very much wants you to be his son-in-law as he promised, but he wants as a price for his daughter the foreskins of one hundred Philistine soldiers." Saul surely thought that in a fierce battle like this David would be killed, and he would be free of a competitor. But David was always up to a challenge, and he encouraged his men to fight their bravest. Not only did they kill one hundred Philistines, they killed two hundred and brought back the foreskins of the two hundred Philistine warriors.

David had fulfilled Saul's requirement, and he came through unscathed. Saul had no choice but to give Michal in marriage to David. So David married her and lived as a member of the king's family.

We are told that an evil spirit came upon Saul. Whether he was a victim of dementia or bipolar disorder, he clearly was no longer rational and David was his target. Amazingly, though, when David played the harp and sang, Saul's mental depression would lift. Imagine what David went through being married to the daughter of a madman who was trying to kill him while he was sitting at the mad king's table. It was a situation that few, if any, would care to endure, but David not only endured it, he continuously prospered.

CHAPTER EIGHT

Abraham—God's Plan for Mankind

We leave now the narrative of David, through whom came the Messiah, to look at God's plan for the human race. Although some geneticists believe that the first human was a woman living in Africa, without question the first human civilization started in what is called Mesopotamia. This word in Greek means "between the rivers." The Tigris and Euphrates rivers flow together into the Persian Gulf. It was here that the first civilization as we know it developed. The area was known as Sumer and had within it the city-states of Eridu, Nippur, Lagash, Uruk, Kish, and Ur. After the flood, when all of the people perished except the family of Noah, new states began to form and their populations grew rapidly. In these city-states, they built pyramids called ziggurats and worshipped a succession of gods and goddesses.

The people of Sumer believed in a creative narrative called *Gilgamesh*, in which Gilgamesh played out their belief in eternal life. Slightly to the north of Sumer was a place called Babylon. It was there that the people attempted to build a tower which would challenge the authority of God Almighty and unite the people against God in a primitive version of a new world order. It was there where God came down and distorted their languages so that the people were no longer able to formulate rebellious plans against Him.

Something else rather strange comes through in the art of a number of disparate civilizations. They are the depictions of demonic beings—fierce-looking creatures, ugly creatures, bizarre-looking creatures. Yet, over all the earth, these nearly identical images are portrayed. Not only was the human race seeking a narrative to explain its existence, but the people also clearly had come to worship demonic beings and to fear them.

In another part of the world, the vast nation of China had developed a creation narrative which involved a mating between Yin and Yang and the resulting offspring that this union produced. However, much more significant to us is the fact that as early as 6,000 BC, the Chinese script *Kanji* reflected the same creation narrative that is found in the Hebrew Bible. For instance, the Kanji for "west" is two people in a garden. The Kanji for an ocean vessel is eight people in a boat. The Kanji for Satan is a man in a tree speaking lies. The Kanji for happiness is a man in the presence of their god who they called Shanti (or Shandi). In fact, the Chinese emperor was said only to be able to rule as long as he could enjoy the "mandate of heaven." In later times, the Emperor performed what was called the border sacrifice, where he ascended the steps to a throne and offered his empire to the god who occupied that throne. On that throne was not a person, but an inscription with the name Shanti (or Shandi). Tiananmen Square in the center of Beijing is supposedly dedicated to the god of heaven who watched over China.

God saw various streams of religious thought coming about and realized that it was necessary for the people who were then living, and the billions who would follow later, that there be a clear understanding of His plan for mankind. He reached into the Mesopotamian civilization and picked a family in Ur headed by a man named Haran and his son, Terah. Terah was the father of a man named Abram. Terah, along with Abram, Abram's wife, and Abram's nephew Lot, journeyed from Ur to a place on the border of what is now known as Syria. At that place,

God spoke to Abram and told him to leave his father's house and go to a land that would be shown to him. He then promised, "I will make you a great nation and … in you all the families of the earth shall be blessed" (Genesis 12:2–3 NKJV). Through this one man, who later was known as Abraham, God began to unfold—and for two thousand years, through a succession of kings, prophets, and holy men—His plan of salvation for the human race that ultimately culminates in the appearance of God's own Son.

The human race had not only seen a revelation of God, but it had been cursed by a number of demonic beings who had been pictured in native art in disparate cultures throughout the globe. God knew that the human race that He had created would not believe His plan of salvation until it was clearly validated over successive years. God chose to entrust the family of Abraham with the true message of salvation, and David became a key figure in the Jewish race to whom God entrusted what were later called the "Oracles of God." This message, which was known first to a small group of people, has now been spread so widely that it has been made available in virtually every tongue and language to the estimated 8 billion people who now inhabit our planet. The concepts of a Creator God, of morality, of prayer, of answers to prayer, of demonic possession, and godly living have all been embedded in the holy Scriptures which are said to be God-breathed.

So, we turn again to David, a man after God's own heart, whom God had placed circa 1,000 BC at the center of the plan of redemption for all of mankind—the shepherd king.

CHAPTER NINE

The Shepherd Boy Becomes King

As Saul's madness deepened, he became more and more obsessed with David's threat to his kingship. He was infuriated because his son Jonathan had formed a strong bond with David. Saul sensed in his spirit that God had taken his blessing from him and transferred it to David. In fact, this is exactly what happened. Here is a summary of that story found in 1 Samuel 16.

God spoke to Samuel and said, "I want you to go to Bethlehem and anoint a successor for Saul." As we know, Samuel had been grieving over Saul's downfall, but he was now ready to move on. So he asked the Lord how he could go to Bethlehem without being observed by Saul and possibly killed by him. So the Lord said, "Take a heifer with you, call the citizens of Bethlehem together, and tell them you have come to sacrifice to the Lord. At the same time, call together Jesse and his sons and I will give you the next part of the plan." Acting in obedience, Samuel went to Bethlehem as he was told and called the family of Jesse together.

One by one, Samuel called Jesse's sons before him. The first was Eliab, and Samuel immediately thought, "He has to be the one God has chosen because he is such a magnificent-looking specimen." He said to the Lord, "Surely this is the one," but

God said, "I am looking at another. Man looks at the outward appearance, but I look at the heart." Then Jesse brought forward his son Abinadab, but he was not the one. Jesse then had his son Shammah pass by, and the Lord said, "Not this one." Jesse had seven of his sons pass before Samuel, but Samuel said, "The Lord has not chosen these." Samuel then inquired of Jesse, "Don't you have any more sons?" And Jesse said, "There is one, the youngest, who is out tending the sheep." Samuel said, "Send for him, because we are not going to sit down to eat until he appears."

When the handsome young man came into the room from the outside, the Lord said, "Rise and anoint him; he is the one."

We are then told that Samuel took the horn of oil and anointed David in the presence of his brothers and from that day forward the Spirit of the Lord God came upon David in power. This transfer of power was unknown to Saul, but the torment in his spirit increased with a vague dread that he was about to lose everything.

As we have learned earlier, David was actually in Saul's employ and was victorious in battle wherever he went. Saul's son Jonathan became David's dear friend, and this friendship deepened Saul's antipathy toward David. David's heart was pure and he bore no ill will against Saul. But David realized the extent of Saul's hatred toward him when one day, while sitting at the dinner table in the palace, Saul hurled a javelin at him. The deepening of Saul's madness and his irrational hatred of David were crystal clear to Jonathan. In fact, Saul screamed at Jonathan, warning him that David was a threat to Jonathan's own future as king of Israel. Jonathan knew that David must flee for his life.

David left the palace and hid in a field. He and Jonathan arranged for a signal that would either tell David he was safe or he should flee as fast as possible. The signal was unmistakable—it was time for David to flee. After a tearful farewell with Jonathan, David fled for his life.

David continued to hide out in the wilderness. While there, he became a rallying point for those in Saul's kingdom who were mistreated or in peril. People came who had been cheated of their property; people came who had been threatened by angry neighbors; people came who owed unjust taxes; and people came who had been fearing arrest. Over time, six hundred men with their families gathered around him. David, the consummate soldier, began to teach them the techniques of warfare. David became like an ancient version of Robin Hood who could take wealth from the unjust rich and give it to the innocent poor. Wherever David and his men were located, there was no fear of brigands, cutthroats, or wild animals. Throughout the Judean countryside, David and his men were heroes.

One wealthy man named Nabal did not share his neighbors' affection for David. It was sheep-shearing time, and Nabal prepared a feast of celebration for his workers and friends. For several years, David and his men had protected Nabal and his property. So naturally, David thought that at a time of celebration, Nabal would show some gratitude for the work that had been done on his behalf. So David sent a couple of men to Nabal to request some of the food at the celebration to be given for his troops. Nabal retorted haughtily, "Who is David? Many men have rebelled against their masters and I have no intention of sharing what is mine with some bandit in the hills." When David heard the news, he was incensed, "I'm going to teach that ingrate a lesson he will never forget." So he ordered his men to strap on their weapons and follow him out of the hills to Nabal's camp. He loudly proclaimed, "When we are finished, there won't be one man alive in Nabal's camp."

When Nabal's wife, Abigail, heard what was in store for her husband and his men, she hurried out to intercept David. She fell at his feet and warned him not to commit acts of vengeance. She flattered him by saying, "Your God has chosen you and will keep you in His protection, but not if you allow this stain to occur in your life." Upon her request, David had a change of heart and thanked her. Then she uttered these words about Nabal, "His name means 'fool,' and he is a fool."

We are told that during the celebration Nabal got staggering drunk. But when he sobered up the next day, Abigail informed him that death and destruction had been narrowly averted. Nabal was so shocked by this news that he suffered a stroke and later died. Upon his death, Abigail and her maids went out to offer themselves as servants to David and his troops. David was so impressed by her beauty and her humble spirit that he asked her to become his wife, an invitation she willingly accepted. This liaison became one of many for David, who had become passionately committed to members of the opposite sex, even as they were passionately attracted to him.

The next years of David's life consisted of a struggle against Saul. Time and again, David had opportunities to kill Saul and end the conflict, but he had a deep-seated respect for the anointing of God on Saul. Though he knew that one day God would end Saul's life, David refused to be the agent of Saul's destruction.

CHAPTER TEN

David's Psalms of Struggle Against Saul

Many of David's psalms reflected his struggle against Saul. Remember that David was one man with a small army around him, and he was being pursued ruthlessly by a leader of a nation and all of the armies that were at the leader's disposal. Many of the psalms reflect David's struggle. And yet, David would not lift a hand against his oppressor, but he turned to the Lord. Consider these psalms that showed his complete trust in the Lord and his prayer to be delivered from those who attempted to kill him.

"LORD, how many are my foes!
How many rise up against me!
Many are saying of me,
'God will not deliver him.'
But you, LORD, are a shield around me,
my glory, the One who lifts my head high."
(Psalm 3:1–3)

"The LORD has heard my cry for mercy;
the LORD accepts my prayer.
All my enemies will be overwhelmed with shame and anguish;
they will turn back and suddenly be put to shame."
(Psalm 6:9–10)

"For look, the wicked bend their bows;
they set their arrows against the strings
to shoot from the shadows
at the upright in heart."
(Psalm 11:2)

"On the wicked he will rain
fiery coals and burning sulfur;
a scorching wind will be their lot."
(Psalm 11:6)

"The cords of death entangled me;
the torrents of destruction overwhelmed me.
The cords of the grave coiled around me;
the snares of death confronted me.
In my distress I called to the Lord;
I cried to my God for help.
From his temple he heard my voice;
my cry came before him, into his ears."
(Psalm 18:4–6)

"As for God, his way is perfect:
The Lord's word is flawless;
he shields all who take refuge in him.
For who is God besides the Lord?
And who is the Rock except our God?
It is God who arms me with strength
and keeps my way secure.
He makes my feet like the feet of a deer;
he causes me to stand on the heights.

He trains my hands for battle;

my arms can bend a bow of bronze.

You make your saving help my shield,

and your right hand sustains me;

your help has made me great.

You provide a broad path for my feet,

so that my ankles do not give way."

(Psalm 18:30–36)

"Contend, LORD, with those who contend with me;

fight against those who fight against me.

Take up shield and armor;

arise and come to my aid.

Brandish spear and javelin

against those who pursue me.

Say to me,

'I am your salvation.'

May those who seek my life

be disgraced and put to shame;

may those who plot my ruin

be turned back in dismay.

May they be like chaff before the wind,

with the angel of the LORD driving them away;

may their path be dark and slippery,

with the angel of the LORD pursuing them."

(Psalm 35:1–6)

David also wrote psalms that had some of the most sublime words of praise to God that we find in any kind of literature. Consider these words, in Psalm 103:1–17.

"Praise the LORD, my soul; all my inmost being,
praise his holy name.
Praise the LORD, my soul, and forget not all his benefits—
who forgives all your sins and heals all your diseases,
who redeems your life from the pit
and crowns you with love and compassion,
who satisfies your desires with good things
so that your youth is renewed like the eagle's.
The LORD works righteousness and justice for all the oppressed.
He made known his ways to Moses,
his deeds to the people of Israel:
The LORD is compassionate and gracious,
slow to anger, abounding in love.
He will not always accuse,
nor will he harbor his anger forever;
he does not treat us as our sins deserve
or repay us according to our iniquities.
For as high as the heavens are above the earth,
so great is his love for those who fear him;
as far as the east is from the west,
so far has he removed our transgressions from us.
As a father has compassion on his children,
so the LORD has compassion on those who fear him;
for he knows how we are formed,
he remembers that we are dust.
The life of mortals is like grass,
they flourish like a flower of the field;
the wind blows over it and it is gone,
and its place remembers it no more.

> But from everlasting to everlasting
> the LORD's love is with those who fear him."

Nowhere in all sacred scripture will anyone find any description of God better than what David used in the Psalms. This is just a sample of the great love that he had for God his Savior. And it is reflected over and over again in this amazing collection of Psalms that we have available in our Bible.

CHAPTER ELEVEN

A Prophetic Insight into a Future Crucifixion

I can imagine that one night while David was meditating on his God, the Holy Spirit came upon him in great power and he saw before his eyes a scene which overwhelmed him.

In the time frame circa 1,000 BC, the people of Israel had no knowledge of death by crucifixion. History records that, in 332 BC, Alexander the Great had, through monumental effort, conquered the city of Tyre. In his anger at the obdurate refusal of the king of Tyre to surrender to him, he crucified approximately two thousand of the men of Tyre. Other than that, crucifixion was not known to the people of Israel.

Yet in his meditation, David saw a man hanging naked on a cross with nails driven into His hands and feet. He saw rough soldiers surrounding this man, gambling for His clothes and His cloak. He saw this man being stretched in agony and being pierced in the side. And then, He uttered, "My God, my God, why have you forsaken me?" These are the very words that David's descendant, Jesus the Messiah, spoke on the cross in Aramaic: *"Eloi, Eloi, lama sabachthani!"*

I imagine David must have been physically weak after this experience, but little did he know that through him, God had described in precise detail the exact description of the death of David's descendant, Jesus of Nazareth, who had been born in the City of David.

Here are the words of David's psalm that can be compared, word for word, with the New Testament account of the crucifixion and death of Jesus Christ:

"My God, my God, why have you forsaken me?

Why are you so far from saving me,

so far from my cries of anguish?

My God, I cry out by day, but you do not answer,

by night, but I find no rest.

Yet you are enthroned as the Holy One;

you are the one Israel praises.

In you our ancestors put their trust;

they trusted and you delivered them.

To you they cried out and were saved;

in you they trusted and were not put to shame.

But I am a worm and not a man,

scorned by everyone, despised by the people.

All who see me mock me;

they hurl insults, shaking their heads.

'He trusts in the LORD,' they say,

'let the LORD rescue him.

Let him deliver him,

since he delights in him.'

Yet you brought me out of the womb;

you made me trust in you, even at my mother's breast.

From birth I was cast on you;

from my mother's womb you have been my God.

Do not be far from me,

for trouble is near

and there is no one to help.
Many bulls surround me;
strong bulls of Bashan encircle me.
Roaring lions that tear their prey
open their mouths wide against me.
I am poured out like water,
and all my bones are out of joint.
My heart has turned to wax;
it has melted within me.
My mouth is dried up like a potsherd,
and my tongue sticks to the roof of my mouth;
you lay me in the dust of death.
Dogs surround me,
a pack of villains encircles me;
they pierce my hands and my feet.
All my bones are on display;
people stare and gloat over me.
They divide my clothes among them
and cast lots for my garment."
(Psalm 22:1–18)

We must realize the incredible significance of Psalm 22. Only God Himself, through the power of the Holy Spirit, could have laid out in precise detail the actual crucifixion of Jesus Christ a thousand years in the future. Without doubt, David was unique among all the great figures of history in this regard.

CHAPTER TWELVE

David and His Descendant Jesus Christ

We should also consider the significance of King David in the life of Jesus Christ. Remember that the term *Christ* was a title which meant "anointed," and *Christos* is the Greek translation of the Hebrew *Mashiach*, "the anointed one." The interplay of David and his descendant Jesus Christ is extraordinary.

In Luke 1:32, we read that an angel named Gabriel came to Nazareth in Galilee. There, a virgin named Mary was espoused to be married to a man named Joseph, a descendant of David. The angel Gabriel told Mary that she would bear a child who would be great and "would be called the Son of the Most High. The Lord will give him the throne of His *father David*." This, of course, means that the prize offered to Jesus Christ, included *the throne of David*. We remember also that the angels who announced the birth of Jesus Christ said, "Today in the City of David is born a savior, which is Christ the Lord."

We ask ourselves, "Why not in the city of Moses—or the City of Samuel—or the City of Elijah?" But no, it was the *City of David*. The throne He would occupy was not the throne of Moses, but the *throne of David*.

Moses led the people out of bondage, but he had no kingdom. In truth, Samuel had no kingdom. Elijah was a great prophet, but he had no kingdom. Elisha had the anointing of the Lord that was a thing of wonder, but he had no kingdom. Only David, who had such a powerful anointing upon him, was also a king.

As we have seen in Israel, the spiritual leader would pour oil on the head of the prospective ruler, and he would be the anointed of the Lord.

Time and again, David showed remarkable respect to those who had received such anointing. In all of the conflict in which he engaged, he refused to lift his hands against his enemy, Saul, whom David referred to as "God's anointed."

CHAPTER THIRTEEN

David Refuses to Kill Saul, Leaving It to God

Consider these two examples of David's restraint and his respect for the anointing.

In 1 Samuel 24, David was hiding in a cave. Saul was so close in pursuit that he actually entered the same cave, but sat inside toward the front to relieve himself. While he was thus engaged, David crept up behind him and cut off a small piece of his garment. His men whispered to him, "Now is your chance. Kill him quickly and your troubles will be over!"

But David replied clearly, "I will not lift my hand against God's anointed." When David went out of the cave after Saul had departed, he called to Saul, "My Lord, the king!" David bowed down and prostrated himself with his face to the ground. He said to Saul, "Why do you listen when men say, 'David is bent on harming you?' Some urge me to kill you, but I will not lift my hand against the LORD's anointed. This day you have seen with your own eyes how the LORD delivered you into my hands in the cave." Saul said, "I understand now that the LORD delivered me into your hands. Does any man treat his enemy as you have treated me? I know that you will surely be king and that the kingdom of Israel will be established in your hands. Now swear to me by the LORD that you will not cut off my descendants or wipe out my name from my father's family." So, David gave his oath to Saul, Saul returned home, and David went back to the stronghold.

In another example from 1 Samuel 26, Saul and his men encamped outdoors and were sound asleep. Saul had placed his spear and water jug at his head before he lay down to sleep. God caused Saul's general, Abner, and his other soldiers to fall into a deep sleep. David boldly crept down to the encampment, picked up the spear and water jug, and moved to a safe place. Then he called out loudly to Abner, "What kind of guard are you, to think you are allowing your king to be placed in peril? I have his spear and water jug. Send one of the young men to come and get it from me." Saul awoke and said, "Is that you, my son David?" And David said, "Yes. Why do you pursue me? I mean you no harm."

Of course, Saul sounded contrite and acknowledged David's honorable nature and compassion and assured him that he would no longer pursue him. David realized there was no real truth to this statement, and he and his men continued their flight away from Saul's army. Despite Saul's promises, David thought to himself, "One of these days I will be destroyed by the hand of Saul. The best thing I can do is escape to the land of the Philistines. Then Saul will give up searching for me anywhere in Israel and I will slip out of his hands." So, David and the 600 men with him left and went to Achish, son of Maok, King of Gath. Each man had his family with him. When Saul was told David had fled to Gath, he no longer searched for him.

Then David said to Achish, "If I have found favor in your eyes, let a place be assigned to me in one of the country towns that I may live there." So on that day, Achish gave him Ziklag, and it has belonged to the kings of Judah ever since.

In those days, David and his men ruthlessly pillaged the surrounding territory of the Geshurites, Girzites, and the Amalekites. He was brutal and left no man or woman alive, but took sheep, cattle, donkeys, camels, and clothes. When he returned to Achish, he told him he had been raiding the towns in the Negev, which were part of Israel. In the process, David had amassed for himself quite a stash of plunder, and this laid the foundation for what in later years became a sizable fortune.

While David was with the Philistines, things were not going well for Saul in Israel. The Philistines gathered a large force on the mountains of Gilboa. Saul attempted to obtain directions from God as to how to proceed with the battle. Nothing was forthcoming. Saul, who was still suffering from mental illness, became terrified at the prospect of the upcoming battle against superior Philistine forces. Since no guidance was forthcoming through the accepted channels, and Samuel had died, Saul disguised himself and went to a place called Endor to visit a witch. We are not sure what powers are real or what are imagined, but we are told that the witch was like a modern-day psychic who could communicate with the dead—in this case, not only communicate but bring them up in bodily form. Not knowing that her customer was indeed King Saul, she said, "Don't you realize that Saul has cut off all of the mediums from the land? Are you trying to trap me?" Saul swore that the woman would receive no punishment if she did as he requested. So, she looked him straight in the eye and asked him, "Who would you like for me to bring up?" And he replied, "Samuel."

But suddenly there appeared an apparition before her, and she screamed out, "You are Saul!" And he again made clear, "No punishment will come upon you." Samuel said, "Why have you disturbed me by bringing me up?" And Saul replied in a trembling voice, "The Philistines are upon me and I can receive no direction as to what I can expect." Samuel replied, "I told you that because of your disobedience, the Lord had taken the kingdom from you and given it to David. Tomorrow, you and your sons will be killed in the battle and you will be with me."

The next day, the Philistines won a great battle on Mount Gilboa. Saul's sons Jonathan, Abinadab, and Malki-Shua were all killed, and he was gravely wounded. In order to hasten his death, Saul fell on his sword and died.

When the Israelites realized that their king was dead, they returned to their towns. The next day when the Philistines visited the battlefield, they found Saul's dead body, took off his armor, cut off his head, and sent it to their capital city.

When the people of Jabesh-Gilead heard what the Philistines had done to Saul, they took down the bodies of Saul and his sons from Beth Shan, and went to Jabesh where they burned them, and then took their bones and buried them under a tamarisk tree, and they fasted for seven days.

CHAPTER FOURTEEN

Warfare Between the Tribes of Benjamin and Judah

Saul and his two principal sons had been killed on Mount Gilboa, but the men of the tribe of Benjamin, and especially their military leaders, had no intention of surrendering the power of kingship.

Saul's surviving son was named Ish-Bosheth, and the leader of the army was Saul's relative, Abner. Abner took Ish-Bosheth and made him king over Gilead, Ashuri, and Jezreel, and also Ephraim, Benjamin, and all Israel. Ish-Bosheth, son of Saul, reigned for two years, but the house of Judah followed David.

The head of David's forces was Joab, who was the son of David's sister, Zeruiah. It would seem that David's choice of military commanders was very much a family affair. His father, Jesse, had eight sons and David was the youngest. David's sisters were Zeruiah and Abigail. Zeruiah's three sons were Abishai, Joab, and Asahel. Abigail was the mother of Amasa. These four cousins all had important positions in David's army.

Joab and Abner met with a small contingent of their armies. Joab suggested, "Why don't we have twelve of each of our troops engage in hand-to-hand combat to see which side will prevail?" What resulted was nothing but a slaughter in which each contestant grabbed his opponent by the beard and thrust him through with his dagger. This minor conflict then triggered a war, and Abner and the forces of Israel were defeated by Joab and David's army. In the process, Joab's brother, Asahel, was killed by Abner, and after a vicious conflict the two sides called a truce and went home.

This opening skirmish led to a long war between the forces led by Abner and the forces loyal to David. While the conflict dragged on, Abner strengthened his own position in the house of Saul until he, in fact, became the true ruler of Israel and Ish-Bosheth was little more than a figurehead.

Now it turned out that Saul had an attractive concubine whose name was Rizpah. Abner was very much attracted to Rizpah and began sleeping with her. One day Abner appeared before Ish-Bosheth who sternly asked him, "Why are you sleeping with my father's concubine?" Powerful generals are very sensitive to receive a rebuke from a puppet king. Abner was no exception. He stormed out of the room, throwing up his hands, and declaring to Ish-Bosheth, "I've given you your kingship and you insult me concerning a woman! It's time that I turn your kingship over to David, the one who God has chosen as leader of His people." But Ish-Bosheth didn't dare answer Abner because he was afraid of him.

Shortly after, Abner traveled to David's headquarters and declared to him, "You are the one chosen by God and I want to pledge my allegiance to you." Abner had brought with him the consent of the leaders of Benjamin. David was delighted with the news and he prepared a great feast for him and his men. Then Abner went throughout Israel to rally support from not only the tribe of Benjamin, but for all of Israel to come and make David king.

While he was engaged in this worthy mission, the commander of David's forces, Joab, heard of it. He realized that Abner was a powerful figure and had more experience than he did, and knew that if Abner went forward with his plan that he (Joab) would be out of a job. Joab lured Abner away from his forces, met him privately, and then stabbed him in the stomach, killing him.

David was heartbroken at the news and not only attended Abner's funeral, but walked behind the casket on the way to the graveyard. From that moment on, there was a struggle between the forces of David and what was left of Saul's supporters whom Abner had sought to bring to David's support.

When Ish-Bosheth was alone one day, two men slipped into his bedroom and assassinated him. Then they hurried to David with the good news. David was incensed and ordered his men to kill these assassins. They cut off their hands and feet and hung their bodies by the pool at Hebron.

The struggle was over and now the men of Israel came to David and said to him, "We are your flesh and blood, and you have been the one to lead the army of Israel successfully." Together they agreed that David would now be their king, and David made a compact with them at Hebron before the Lord.

In the Bible, thirty years was the age when Levites became priests and when kings were given their leadership. David was no exception. He was thirty years old when he became king, and he reigned for forty years. In Hebron, he reigned over Judah for seven years and six months, and in Jerusalem he reigned over all Israel and Judah thirty-three years.

CHAPTER FIFTEEN

Bethlehem, City of David

Bethlehem in Judea was called the City of David. David's family came from Bethlehem, and David was anointed king in Bethlehem. The name Bethlehem means "house of bread" or "house of food." David was born in that city approximately 1,085 BC.

In later years, the Israelite farmers had learned exacting agricultural techniques. Their land area was relatively modest—about 3,000–5,000 square meters. The transfer of land was extremely important and intricate regulations had been established to determine inheritance.

Over hundreds of years, successive waves of invaders cut down the abundant forests of Israel and left many parts of the land dry and desolate. This, however, was not the case during David's lifetime. The land of Israel has been described as a "land of milk and honey." One of the symbols of modern-day Israel depicts the two Israelite spies who were carrying a branch on their shoulders from which descended an enormous cluster of grapes, reflecting the abundance of the Promised Land that God was to give to His people.

Here is a description by a Roman historian writing circa 300 AD: "Many aggadot [legends] celebrate the abundance and fertility of the land of Israel and mention grape clusters as large as oxen; mustard as tall as fig trees; two radishes being a full load for a camel; turnips large enough to constitute a fox's den; a peach large enough to feed a man to satiety" (Jewish Virtual Library, https://www.jewishvirtuallibrary.org/history-and-overview-of-agriculture-in-israel).

Whether these fantastic quantities of produce existed in the time of David, we don't know, but we feel certain that Bethlehem was an extraordinarily wealthy agricultural city located a short distance from Jerusalem. We can imagine that during David's time there were bustling markets and an abundance of produce, grain, wine, olive oil, and multiple varieties of fruit and vegetables.

In previous years, Bethlehem was a Christian village whose mayor, Elias Freij, ran a small business manufacturing olive wood ornaments. Bethlehem was later taken over by Yasser Arafat and the PLO. But despite the turmoil, it is still the site of the Christmas narrative of a baby born in a manger, angels appearing to shepherds, visits by wise men, and a beautiful Christmas carol, "O Little Town of Bethlehem."

Although the shepherd was now king, his battles were not over as we learn as this narrative continues.

CHAPTER SIXTEEN

David's Standard of Conduct

David's psalms were primarily written in glorification of his walk with God. They were songs of praise and worship. But at least two of them point to the strict morality that governed his life and what he perceived as the ideal standards of a holy God.

In Psalm 15, David raises the question of, "Who can live with the Lord on His holy hill?"

> "Lord, who may dwell in your sacred tent?
> Who may live on your holy mountain?
> The one whose walk is blameless,
> who does what is righteous,
> who speaks the truth from their heart;
> whose tongue utters no slander,
> who does no wrong to a neighbor,
> and casts no slur on others;
> who despises a vile person
> but honors those who fear the Lord;
> who keeps an oath even when it hurts,
> and does not change their mind;
> who lends money to the poor without interest;

who does not accept a bribe against the innocent.

Whoever does these things

will never be shaken."

(Psalm 15)

Psalm 101 reflected David's own personal conflict in his home when no one was watching, and in his kingship.

"I will sing of your love and justice;

to you, Lord, I will sing praise.

I will be careful to lead a blameless life—

when will you come to me?

I will conduct the affairs of my house

with a blameless heart.

I will not look with approval

on anything that is vile.

I hate what faithless people do;

I will have no part in it.

The perverse of heart shall be far from me;

I will have nothing to do with what is evil.

Whoever slanders their neighbor in secret,

I will put to silence;

whoever has haughty eyes and a proud heart,

I will not tolerate.

My eyes will be on the faithful in the land,

that they may dwell with me;

the one whose walk is blameless

will minister to me.

No one who practices deceit

will dwell in my house;

no one who speaks falsely

will stand in my presence.

Every morning I will put to silence

all the wicked in the land;

I will cut off every evildoer

from the city of the LORD."

(Psalm 101)

These are principles that have lived through the ages and reflect a remarkably high standard for us today.

Consider this, "I will not look with approval on anything that is vile" (Psalm 101:3). How often are our eyes focused on television programs that are essentially vile, filled with murder, adultery, incest, and crime? Consider the books that are available, almost all of which are vile in one way or the other. Who among us can say we have not read something or watched something that could, indeed, be classified as vile—not pornographic or filthy—but just vile?

We read in Psalm 15:1–3, "Who may live on your holy mountain? … Whose tongue utters no slander, who does no wrong to a neighbor, and casts no slur on others?" Our focus is so often on sexual sins and such things as divorce, bigamy, adultery, etc. But we, as Christians, blithely slander one another or people with whom we disagree as if such statements are not morally wrong. In truth, there is no ranking of sins between mortal, venial, and so-called peccadillos. Slander is slander. Character assassination is character assassination. Calling someone a fool is a sin. Trying to belittle a neighbor is wrong. David goes on to say in Psalm 101:5, "Whoever has haughty eyes and a proud heart, I will not tolerate." Taken together, these two psalms give a perfect blueprint for the type of conduct that should be normative for the people of God.

When these psalms of David are coupled with the Golden Rule of Jesus Christ and the words of the Apostle Paul in certain epistles of his, we have a moral framework that is much more extensive than the often-repeated command "to act justly and to love mercy and to walk humbly with your God" (Micah 6:8).

Just think how much happier a world we would have if a man's word was his bond, if people spoke truth to their neighbor in love, and if a person's reputation was safe from slander among fellow believers.

Regrettably, in his later life, David failed to follow his own guidance. However, certainly as a young man, these psalms reflect his own inner purity and the standards of conduct which he established for himself and for those in his official household.

CHAPTER SEVENTEEN

Miraculous Zion

After David was named king over Israel, he was faced with a very serious challenge. Within the City of Jerusalem (which was controlled by the Jebusites), was the fortress known as Zion, located at the center of the city. The Jebusites were so secure in their stronghold that they boasted even the lame and blind would be sufficient to defend their stronghold.

Jerusalem lay at a key point close to Bethlehem. David, of necessity, had to conquer it, but how was he to go against such an impregnable fortress? He found a waterway that led into the citadel, and his men crawled up the waterway and then burst upon the Jebusites and quickly took control of the city. It was then called the City of David, and Mount Zion became his headquarters.

Now came the interesting part. Over the years, Zion became synonymous with Israel, and what was first the City of David was, in later writings, merged with the Temple Mount, and together they became known as Zion.

In Isaiah 14:32, the prophet Isaiah says, "The Lord has established Zion." And there are at least fifty references to Zion in the Psalms, such as: "From Zion, perfect in beauty, God shines forth" (Psalm 50:2).

"May it please you to prosper Zion, to build up the walls of Jerusalem" (Psalm 51:18).

The City of David and Mount Zion were one together. However, over the centuries Mount Moriah, or the Temple Mount, became merged with the City of David and Mount Zion. So, together they became known as Mount Zion. Later the combined entity was called Zion and it became another name for the nation of Israel itself. This is found in the writings of a number of prophets, such as Jeremiah, who wrote, "Is the LORD not in Zion? Is her King no longer there?" (Jeremiah 8:19).

But Zion was not merely something mentioned by the prophets. In looking back at the practices of the Old Testament, the New Testament author of the Book of Hebrews mentions that people who approached the holy mountain, Sinai, were in danger of being struck dead. The writer then juxtaposes the heavenly vision for the New Testament in these words from Hebrews 12:22–24: "But you have come to Mount Zion, to the city of the living God, the heavenly Jerusalem. You have come to thousands upon thousands of angels in joyful assembly, to the church of the firstborn, whose names are written in heaven. You have come to God, the Judge of all, to the spirits of the righteous made perfect, to Jesus the mediator of a new covenant, and to the sprinkled blood that speaks a better word than the blood of Abel." And in Hebrews 12:28–29, "Therefore, since we are receiving a kingdom that cannot be shaken, let us be thankful, and so worship God acceptably with reverence and awe, for our 'God is a consuming fire.'"

I remember as a little child singing a song, "We're marching to Zion, beautiful, beautiful Zion. We're marching upward to Zion, the beautiful City of God."

So, we can conclude, the effects of David the Shepherd King are felt throughout history, and in the minds of many, his kingdom has become a symbol of heaven itself.

The Bible was written in two ancient languages. The Old Testament was written in Hebrew, and the New Testament was written in Greek. Unlike modern English, Hebrew and Greek verbs have different tenses to convey meaning. For example, in the Greek New Testament, Jesus tells His disciples to "ask, seek, and knock." These verbs are in the present tense which means continuing action, in this case, keep on asking, keep on seeking, keep on knocking.

If, on the other hand, the verb had been given in the *aorist* tense, it would mean a knock at one time. A great deal of confusion has resulted in inaccurate translation of these words. For example, we are told, "He that is born of God does not sin." However, the word again here is present tense meaning, "He that is born of God does not keep on sinning."

Perhaps the greatest confusion comes about when we find that the phrase "blasphemy against the Holy Spirit" is given in the aorist tense, which in this case means at one time. Yet, we have to believe that only a continuous sin against God's Spirit, which is rejection of Jesus Christ, would be eternal condemnation. We leave this discussion to the theologians and return to the Hebrew language.

In the Hebrew language, the name for God is the Tetragrammaton *YHWH*. It does not display the vowel markings used in Hebrew and, therefore, cannot be translated with absolute certainty. God identified Himself to Moses as *I am that I am*. He is "being" itself. Also particular to Hebrew is the *hyphal* tense, which indicates causation. In the opinion of many commentators, of whom I am one, the name of God is in the *hiphil* tense which means, "He who causes everything to be." The word for *God* (and *angel*) in the Hebrew language is *Elohim*. The word for *my LORD*, or *governor*, is *Adonai*. If the vowels from those words are added to YHWH, we get *Yehowah* (commonly shortened to *Yahweh*) which, we know as *Jehovah*.

Obviously, David did not care about linguistic niceties. His praise was to the Author and Creator of the universe. But keep in mind that in today's Bible translations, we see *LORD*. We realize that *LORD* is a name, not merely a title. And the commandment "not to take the name of the LORD your God in vain" does not refer to the word *God* or to the word *ruler*, but to the holy name of God Himself, which in the *hiphil* sense of the Hebrew verb *to be*, is better translated as "He who causes everything to be."

David has been identified as the servant of Yahweh, and in his battles he asked specifically for direction and received detailed instruction. For instance, the Philistines had a huge force looking to attack David. David asked Yahweh if he should attack the Philistines and if Yahweh would hand them over to him. The answer was, "Go, for I will surely hand the Philistines over to you." So David attacked and won a signal victory.

Apparently, the Philistines were very persistent. They had superior forces and they had no intention of giving up control of Israel. So this time we are told they spread out in the Valley of Rephaim. This time the Lord gave David specific instruction (2 Samuel 5:24): "As soon as you hear the sound of marching in the tops of the poplar trees, move quickly, because that will mean the LORD has gone out in front of you to strike the Philistine army."

So, David spread his forces around the Philistine army, and when he heard the sound of marching, he launched a full-scale attack which resulted in such a slaughter of the Philistines that they withdrew from him. The second book of Samuel 5:25 states clearly: "So David did as the LORD commanded him, and he struck down the Philistines all the way from Gibeon to Gezer."

With a full fighting force at his disposal and the power of God with him, no army could stand before David.

We read that in the course of time, David defeated the Moabites who became subject to David and, "Moreover, David defeated Hadadezer son of Rehob, king of Zobah, when he went to restore his monument at the Euphrates River" (2 Samuel 8:3).

During David's time there was no Geneva Convention nor was there any acceptable conduct as to the treatment of captive prisoners. There were no prisoner-of-war camps. Perhaps if captured troops were left alive, they would go back and rejoin their armies before the battle was over. However, we read in 2 Samuel these words: "David also defeated the Moabites. He made them lie down on the ground and measured them off with a length of cord. Every two lengths of them were put to death, and the third length was allowed to live" (2 Samuel 8:2).

In our 21st-century world, we are filled with horror when we read of the beheadings that take place at the hands of a group like ISIS, or the Taliban in Afghanistan. And here was David, "a man after God's own heart," who made his captives lie down, measured them off with a piece of rope, then killing two out of three of the hapless prisoners thus measured by his technique. It's amazing to readers today that the Bible itself does not attempt some explanation of this barbaric conduct. This type of behavior may have been acceptable in David's time, but today it seems reprehensible.

Suffice it to say, David was an incredibly successful general and, with God's help, won repeated victories. For example, when the Arameans of Damascus came to help Hadadezer, David struck down twenty-two thousand of them and then put garrisons in Damascus. He subdued Edom and Moab, the Ammonites, the Philistines, and the Amalekites.

David became famous after he returned from striking down eighteen thousand Edomites in the Valley of Salt. We are told that the Lord gave David victory wherever he went and what he did was just and right for all of his people.

We also learn that David was a brilliant administrator. He set up his army in divisions of twenty-four thousand men for each month of the year, and appointed officers over the tribes of Israel. He put treasurers and other officers in charge of the finances of the nation and had judges who administered the civil affairs. He had a group of advisors as his personal counsel, and then he set individuals over the management of his personal estates. From what we have learned, the whole nation enjoyed peace and civility.

Instead of a half-crazed king, the people now had a wise, just ruler who we are told led his people with skillful hands (Psalm 78:72). David's fame grew throughout that region, and when Hiram, king of Tyre, heard about what David had done, he sent cedar logs and carpenters and stone masons to build a palace for David. David knew that the Lord had established him as king over Israel and had exalted his kingdom for the sake of His people Israel.

Along with all of his military victories and wise governance, David did not neglect his attraction to members of the opposite sex. In addition to the Lord having given Saul's wives to David, we are told in 2 Samuel 5:13, that "after he left Hebron, David took more concubines and wives in Jerusalem, and more sons and daughters were born to him."

CHAPTER EIGHTEEN

A Fateful Spring Break

In the course of time, the king of the Ammonites died, and his son, Hanun, succeeded him as king. So, David thought he would express sympathy to Hanun concerning his father. He sent a delegation to the son with his warmhearted message. However, when the delegation arrived at the palace of Hanun, his officials came to him with these words: "Do you honestly believe that this delegation is here on a peace mission? No, it is not. These men are here to spy out your land to prepare the way for a military attack against your kingdom." So Hanun disregarded David's gracious overture and instead seized his envoys and humiliated them by shaving off their beards, cutting off their garments in the middle of the buttocks, and then sending them away. When David heard of it, he was incensed. He sent his envoys some fresh clothes and told them to remain at Jericho until their beards had grown back.

David was not the kind of person to let an insult of this nature go unpunished. The Ammonites soon realized that they had stuck a stick in a hornet's nest and that swift retaliation was on the way. So, they sent word to the surrounding kings to hire some mercenary soldiers to fight on their behalf. They hired twenty thousand Aramean foot soldiers from Beth Rehob and Zobah, as well as the king of Maakah with one thousand men, and also twelve thousand men from Tob.

When David learned what the enemy was doing, he ordered Joab to take his army and engage them in battle. Joab split his forces so that one branch could fight the Arameans and one branch could fight the Ammonites.

When Joab and his troops advanced against the Arameans, they fled before him. Soon after, the Ammonites realized they were alone. Then Joab called on David, who mobilized the entire army of Israel to do battle against the Arameans. Here again, the hostile armies fled before David. David's army killed seven hundred of their charioteers and forty thousand of their foot soldiers. He also struck down Shobak, the commander of their army.

When all the kings realized that they were defeated, they made peace with David and became subject to him, and we are told that the Arameans were afraid to help the Ammonites anymore. This, for David, was a magnificent victory. He and his armies had overcome a powerful force in a war that began because of an insult by Hanun, an inexperienced king. Whatever the cause, it was devastation to the Ammonites and the Arameans, and David earned a much-needed rest.

But here becomes the danger. So often after a great victory, fatigue sets in and the victorious one begins to relax, opening the door for attack. This spiritual attack was played out many times in biblical days, and it has been repeated many times in modern days. In modern-day warfare an accepted doctrine is for troops to dig in after a victory and prepare for a counterattack by the enemy. Sadly, this is not what David did. In David's case, it's easy to understand his frame of mind. His army had defeated a major coalition that came against him, and he certainly did not wish to take on another military venture.

The Bible records that it was spring, "the time when kings go to war." But David stayed behind in the palace. In truth, in spiritual warfare, there is no such thing as a "rest area," nor is there any place to hide.

Like it or not, God's people are always on the front line, although from time to time, they have a much-needed rest as long as they remain spiritually vigilant.

Regrettably, David had not learned this valuable spiritual lesson. He wisely refrained from undertaking another major battle and was enjoying a much-needed rest. It was a beautiful time of year and he was on the balcony of his palace enjoying the evening.

As David looked at an adjoining property, his eyes fastened upon a beautiful young woman. We were reminded of the statement of Job, who said in justification of his own suffering, "I made a covenant with mine own eyes not to look upon a maid." Unfortunately for David, he looked once—and then he looked again. And before his eyes was an absolutely gorgeous, naked woman bathing.

We remind ourselves that David was king and he had at his disposal several wives and many concubines. They were all his, and he could have satisfied any sexual urges with a legitimate liaison with one of these women. Instead, he wanted the one who belonged to someone else.

So he called his aides and said, "Go get that woman for me." They brought her to him and David learned her name was Bathsheba (which means "daughter of an oath"). Being the king, he ordered her into his bed chamber and had sex with her. She went back to her dwelling and, after a couple of months, realized that she had been impregnated by him and was now carrying his child. So she sent word to David, "I am pregnant."

In many instances, the cover-up is worse than the sin itself. Instead of admitting that he had taken another man's wife and impregnated her, he decided the best idea would be a cover-up. He would bring her husband, Uriah, who was fighting with the army under the command of Joab, home so that he would have sex with his wife and could then have the baby attributed to him.

Uriah was at the core of David's fighting men, being one of the thirty warriors who formed David's bodyguard. When Uriah came before David as he had been instructed to do, David received from his hand the field dispatch from Joab and then said to Uriah, "Go home and visit your wife." But Uriah was so righteous that he said to himself, "How can I go to my dwelling and drink and eat good food and then lie with my wife while my compatriots are eating field rations, lying on the cold ground, and engaged in warfare?" So, he refused to go home. Of course, David thought he had come up with the perfect solution to his problem, and now this member of his bodyguard was frustrating his plan. So, he tried every artifice available to him including getting Uriah drunk, but Uriah steadfastly refused to perform as expected.

In the Book of Ecclesiastes we read, "Do not be righteous over much." Though Uriah thought that his conduct was extremely righteous, he had established his own standard of righteousness, and this led to his untimely death. Everyone should beware of setting standards of conduct which are not specifically mandated by Scripture. Marriages have been torn apart, churches have been ripped apart, friendships have been torn apart, businesses have been torn apart—all because one of the participants has set up standards of perceived righteousness which are of their devising, but do not come from God Himself. Uriah, Bathsheba's husband, had set up a concept of righteousness, which ultimately cost him his life.

David realized that Uriah had no intention of going along with David's proposal, so he decided to have him killed. He wrote a letter, sealed it, and gave it to Uriah to take back to Joab. In the letter, David instructed, "When the action is most fierce, put Uriah on the point and then withdraw from him." When that did happen, Uriah was surrounded by enemy soldiers and killed by their hand. Joab reported on the action and told David not to be angry, that the troops had gotten too close to the wall and some had been killed including his servant, Uriah.

When news of Uriah's death reached David, he told Bathsheba that her husband had been killed, and she was free to become his wife. David took her, and she lived with him as his wife from then on. In the solemn commentary, the record has these words, "But the thing David had done displeased the LORD."

The LORD sent Nathan to David. When he came to him, he said, "There were two men in a certain town, one rich and the other poor. The rich man had a very large number of sheep and cattle, but the poor man had nothing except one little ewe lamb he had bought. He raised it, and it grew up with him and his children. It shared his food, drank from his cup and even slept in his arms. It was like a daughter to him.

Now a traveler came to the rich man, but the rich man refrained from taking one of his own sheep or cattle to prepare a meal for the traveler who had come to him. Instead, he took the ewe lamb that belonged to the poor man and prepared it for the one who had come to him." David burned with anger against the man and said to Nathan, "As surely as the LORD lives, the man who did this must die! He must pay for that lamb four times over, because he did such a thing and had no pity." Then Nathan said to David, "You are the man! This is what the LORD, the God of Israel, says: 'I anointed you king over Israel, and I delivered you from the hand of Saul. I gave your master's house to you, and your master's wives into your arms. I gave you all Israel and Judah. And if all this had been too little, I would have given you even more. Why did you despise the word of the LORD by doing what is evil in his eyes? You struck down Uriah the Hittite with the sword and took his wife to be your own. You killed him with the sword of the Ammonites.

Now, therefore, the sword will never depart from your house, because you despised me and took the wife of Uriah the Hittite to be your own.' This is what the LORD says: 'Out of your own household I am going to bring calamity on you.'" (2 Samuel 12:1–11)

David had taken Bathsheba as his wife, and the child that she conceived with David grew sickly and died. Then we are told David comforted his wife, Bathsheba, and she conceived and bore a child who was named Solomon.

Despite David's marital difficulties, Joab, the commander of his army, continued to wage war against the capital of the Ammonites. So David went out and commanded the army, captured Rabbah, and took the Ammonite crown and placed it on his head as a sign of victory. But the trouble which the Lord had promised was still to unfold with terrible ferocity.

CHAPTER NINETEEN

Rape and Murder among David's Children

Over the passing of time, David's children reached their late teens and early twenties and began to assert themselves. Although they were all David's children, with a few exceptions, they were children of different wives, and they were, therefore, not full brothers or sisters. We learn Amnon, one of David's sons, fell in love with Tamar who was the beautiful full sister of Absalom who was also the son of David. Amnon was frustrated to the point of sickness because Tamar was a virgin and seemingly had no interest in having sexual relations with him.

His advisor was a man named Jonadab, son of Shimeah, David's brother. So when Amnon told him, "I'm in love with Tamar, my brother Absalom's sister." Jonadab said, "Here is the plan. Go to bed, pretend to be sick, and ask the king to let Tamar come and prepare food for you in your sickness."

Tamar did as she had been instructed and entered the supposed sick room of her half-brother. He then ordered the attendants to leave them alone and then over-powered this young virgin and raped her. She cried out to him, "Don't do this, my brother. If you ask the king, he will give me to you as a wife." But Amnon refused to listen, and he raped his half-sister.

When the rape was over, Amnon's sexual desire turned to hatred, and he ordered his attendants to thrust Tamar out from his quarters. She loudly wailed that this affront was worse than the rape, and she tore her clothes and went out crying loudly. When her brother, Absalom, learned what had happened, he vowed in his heart that he would kill Amnon for this crime against his sister.

Two years later, Absalom was having a party to celebrate the shearing of his sheep, and he invited King David to come as his guest. David realized what a burden it would be for his son to host the king and his royal entourage, so he replied to Absalom, "No, my son, I will be a burden to you. You enjoy the festival." Then Absalom said, "Please allow my brothers to attend the festival, especially Amnon." So, all the brothers gathered together at Absalom's festival.

However, unbeknownst to King David, Absalom had given orders to his servants for them to kill Amnon at the height of the festivity. So, when the family was eating and drinking and celebrating Absalom's good fortune, his servants suddenly fell upon Amnon and murdered him. When this was done, the brothers exited as soon as possible, jumped on their mules, and rode away.

The word reached David that all of his sons had been killed by Absalom, and he fell weeping to the ground. But Jonadab assured him that only Amnon had been killed because he had raped Absalom's sister.

Indeed, when the sons returned to the palace, David was encouraged that only Amnon had been killed, but he mourned for Absalom who had fled to Talmai, son of Ammihud, the king of Geshur. Absalom stayed there for three years and we are told that David mourned the absence of Absalom more than he did the death of Amnon.

At this point, it is difficult to understand what went on in Absalom's mind. He was obviously the favorite among the king's sons. But during his three-year absence, what should have been loyalty toward his father turned into bitter resentment. Instead of love, there grew intense hatred. Day after day, as he mused on his hatred of his brothers and his father, he conceived a plan that would take away the kingship from David and transfer it to himself. So, step by step, he began to carry out a diabolical plot which ultimately led to a rebellion of the nation of Israel against his own father.

CHAPTER TWENTY

Absalom Plans Regicide and Patricide

There are many motivations which bring about behavior such as Absalom exhibited. In fact, the first sin was committed by the most beautiful of God's creations, Lucifer, whose task was to cover the very holiness of God. As Lucifer considered his own beauty and his own wisdom, he determined in his mind that he could do a better job running the whole universe than was done by God the Creator. In what could be considered the first sin, Lucifer's pride led him to revolt against God and take a third of the angels with him. This was the first evidence of sin in the universe, and its cause was pride.

Undoubtedly, Absalom had that same type of pride with which he convinced himself that he could do a better job of running the kingdom of Israel than his father, David, had been doing. But there was more in his complicated and fevered brain. He was a murderer, and for this crime he had never been punished. He had been in exile for three years and, through the urging of General Joab, had been allowed to return to the palace. While there, the king initially refused to give him an audience, but after some time he was free to mingle among the people. He did not, however, enjoy the warmth of his father's love to which he felt he was entitled.

Since his father was the ultimate authority, perhaps Absalom believed that if his father was dead, there would be no further punishment or isolation for his crime.

There are two sins, one called *regicide*, which means killing the ruler, the other *patricide*, which means killing one's father. In his bitterness, Absalom was more and more willing to kill his own father who was the king of Israel. His planning belied the fact of his name, Absalom—which means "father of peace"—*av shalom*.

He planned very carefully how he would go about his nefarious mission. Whenever people would come seeking an audience with the king, he intercepted them and kissed them saying, "If only I were king I would be happy to hear your complaint and ensure that you receive justice." Day by day, as people came seeking an audience with his father, David, Absalom intercepted them with this friendly appeal. It took him a couple of years to accomplish his task, but the record shows that, "Absalom won the hearts of the people."

His next move was to organize a fighting force that would be capable of storming the palace and killing the king. But David's advisors learned of Absalom's plot and warned David that he must flee Jerusalem before his son was able to kill him.

We are given a mournful spectacle of the great man, David, walking barefoot out of Jerusalem with a couple of squadrons of fighting men and being pelted by a Benjamite relative of Saul, Shimei, who hurled dust at him along with vile curses.

When one of David's fighting men watched this spectacle, he said to David, "Your majesty, why don't I take off this dog's head?" But David replied, "This is the Lord's curse upon me. So, leave Shimei alone and let him curse."

When David reached the crest of the hill outside of Jerusalem, he learned that his wise counselor, Ahithophel, had gone over to Absalom's camp. David uttered a prayer, "Lord, throw confusion into the counsel of Ahithophel."

About that time, Hushai, drew abreast of him and said, "Your majesty, I want to come with you." And David said, "No, my friend, you would just be a burden on the way. Go back and offer advice to my rebel son, Absalom."

CHAPTER TWENTY-ONE

Thousands Die on Densely Wooded Battlefield

Absalom and his forces had moved into the palace and the question was how to legitimize Absalom's overthrow of his father and, at the same time, determine what course of action should be taken to defeat him militarily. So the question was raised as to how the people of Israel would know that Absalom had really humiliated David to such an extent that only a war could take power away from him now.

Ahithophel came forward with this advice to Absalom, "Go up to the roof of the palace and spread a tent there. Then have sex with David's concubines in the sight of all Israel. Then they will realize that you are in charge of Israel and have made an irrevocable break with your father." So, indeed a tent was spread on the roof of the palace, and Absalom went in and had sex with a number of David's concubines.

It's amazing how the Bible characterizes this particular action, and praises Ahithophel, saying that he was so wise: "It was as if his words were coming directly from God Himself."

Then Absalom asked his advisors what should be done next to ensure the death of his father, David. The first to speak was Ahithophel who said, "David is tired now and has a small force of fighting men with him. My counsel is that you take your army and attack him quickly before he is able to cross the Jordan, and when you do you will have won the victory that you were seeking."

Then Absalom turned to Hushai who had joined him. Absalom did not realize that Hushai was David's agent. Hushai gave this counsel: "We know that your father is a skilled warrior. He is off hidden in some cave now, out of reach of your army. If there is a fight and some of your troops are killed, a panic will set in among your remaining troops and your battle will be lost. I recommend that you mobilize the entire army of Israel, and you lead it into battle. Wherever David has hidden himself, go there and threaten to tear the walls down if need be, but you will surely prevail."

After deliberation, the royal counsel said, "The counsel of Hushai is better than that of Ahithophel." Absalom agreed. The biblical records then declare, "The Lord had determined to defeat the counsel of Ahithophel and to frustrate Absalom's plot."

Ahithophel went from the meeting in disgrace and committed suicide. In doing so, he removed from Absalom's counsel the wisest advisor then available to him, because God in His wisdom had no intention of permitting His servant, David, to be killed by this wayward son.

Hushai told Zadok and Abiathar, the priests, of the advice that was given, and urged them to hurry to David to warn him not to spend a night in the desert, but to cross over the Jordan with the troops available to him.

So during the night, David and all of his men crossed safely out of reach of Absalom and his forces. David now had time to regroup his troops and placed one third of the contingent under the command of Joab, a third under Joab's brother, Abishai, and a third under Ittai the Gittite. David offered to march at the head of the troops, but his commanders would not permit him to risk his life in the upcoming dangerous battle. Absalom chose Amasa, who happened to be a first cousin of Joab, to command the forces of Israel.

King David watched as his forces marched out in units of hundreds and thousands. To his leaders, David gave this command, "In the battle, be gentle with my son Absalom." They all heard the king's words, but Joab had a hard time believing them. He realized what was at stake, and he had no intention of sparing Absalom if an opportunity arose to terminate his life.

The battle took place between David's troops and the troops loyal to Absalom. The battlefield was not a smooth plain, but a densely wooded area. We are told that the battle was so intense that the army of Israel suffered twenty thousand casualties, but more people died because of the thick forest than they did in actual combat.

In the heat of battle, Absalom was riding on a mule. His head of hair was so thick that when it was cut occasionally, the cuttings alone were said to weigh a total of five pounds. His mule ran under a tree and Absalom's thick head of hair got caught in the branches of a tree. He was left hanging helpless. When Joab saw him, he demanded of the troops, "Why didn't you finish him off?" To which the troops replied, "We heard the statement of the king and tried to be obedient to what he requested." Joab—an arrogant general who had not hesitated to murder in cold blood a couple of his rivals—took three darts and thrust them into Absalom's heart, thereby killing him.

Then Joab sounded a trumpet and halted the battle. They took Absalom, threw him in a big pit, and piled rocks over him. Meanwhile, the rest of Israel's army fled the scene and went to their homes.

David was sitting beside the gates of the town he had occupied, eagerly awaiting news of the battle. Ahimaaz son of Zadok said, "Let me run with the news." And Joab permitted him. He then picked an Ethiopian with the full story to run as well. When David saw them coming, he welcomed the news. Ahimaaz arrived first, but was unable to tell David the fate of Absalom. So David instructed him to stand aside, and when the Ethiopian came, David said, "What is the news of the young man, Absalom?" The Ethiopian replied, "Let all the enemies of the king be as that young man is today." Instead of being joyful, David was heartbroken, and he began to moan, "Oh, my son, my son. If only it had been me and not you."

It's hard for us to imagine a more loving and compassionate father than David. Here was the son who had rebelled against him, the son who gladly would have murdered him, the son who tried to tear his kingdom away from him—and yet David was mourning over his death.

So instead of rejoicing over a victory that had saved the kingship for David, the troops began to slink away in disgrace. General Joab came to David and said in effect, "What is the matter with you? These men have saved your kingdom and the future of your dynasty. If you fail to congratulate them over the victory you have won at great sacrifice, you will have no army left and your situation will be worse than it has ever been." So David took a seat at the city gate and the men came to him. He warmly congratulated them and thanked them for the victory they had won for him—the victory which had saved the kingdom.

CHAPTER TWENTY-TWO

David Asks Forgiveness for Adultery and Murder

Was the revolt of Absalom, the shocking waste of life, and the near loss of everything he counted dear God's punishment on David for his adulterous affair with Bathsheba and the murder of her husband, Uriah? Probably so. As often is the case, we must learn that God, in His infinite love, will take away the eternal consequences of our actions, but will leave in place the temporal consequences which can be very painful to us. Unlike Saul, David showed his great contrition for what he had done. He spelled it out in great detail in Psalm 51 where we read these words:

> "Have mercy on me, O God,
> according to your unfailing love;
> according to your great compassion
> blot out my transgressions.
> Wash away all my iniquity
> and cleanse me from my sin.
> For I know my transgressions,
> and my sin is always before me.
> Against you, you only, have I sinned
> and done what is evil in your sight;
> so you are right in your verdict

and justified when you judge.

Surely I was sinful at birth,

sinful from the time my mother conceived me.

Yet you desired faithfulness even in the womb;

you taught me wisdom in that secret place.

Cleanse me with hyssop, and I will be clean;

wash me, and I will be whiter than snow.

Let me hear joy and gladness;

let the bones you have crushed rejoice.

Hide your face from my sins

and blot out all my iniquity.

Create in me a pure heart, O God,

and renew a steadfast spirit within me.

Do not cast me from your presence

or take your Holy Spirit from me.

Restore to me the joy of your salvation

and grant me a willing spirit, to sustain me.

Then I will teach transgressors your ways,

so that sinners will turn back to you.

Deliver me from the guilt of bloodshed, O God,

you who are God my Savior,

and my tongue will sing of your righteousness.

Open my lips, Lord,

and my mouth will declare your praise.

You do not delight in sacrifice, or I would bring it;

you do not take pleasure in burnt offerings.

My sacrifice, O God, is a broken spirit;

a broken and contrite heart

you, God, will not despise.

> May it please you to prosper Zion,
>
> to build up the walls of Jerusalem.
>
> Then you will delight in the sacrifices of the righteous,
>
> in burnt offerings offered whole;
>
> then bulls will be offered on your altar."

Again, consider these two verses (Psalm 51:10–12) as being normative for Christians today:

> Create in me a pure heart, O God,
>
> and renew a steadfast spirit within me.
>
> Do not cast me from your presence
>
> or take your Holy Spirit from me.
>
> Restore to me the joy of your salvation
>
> and grant me a willing spirit, to sustain me.

When a person sins, according to this psalm, the joy of salvation departs from them until such time as they confess and forsake what they have been doing. At the same time, however, the Holy Spirit is not taken from them, so the concept of "losing salvation" does not take place merely because of sin, even sin as heinous as adultery and murder. The joy lifts, but the power of the Holy Spirit remains. So again, David's words resound… "Restore to me the joy of your salvation and grant me a willing spirit, to sustain me."

CHAPTER TWENTY-THREE

Sheba's Revolt

We realize that Absalom's revolt had completely torn the Kingdom of Israel apart. The citizens of Judah had remained loyal to David, but many citizens of other tribes had joined with Absalom. Now that the rebellion was over, the whole nation wanted their king back, although there was some dispute between Judah and the rest of Israel. A consensus was forming to put David back on the throne.

A troublemaker named Sheba, son of Bikri, a Benjamite, sounded the trumpet and said, "We have no share in David." Clearly this rebellion had to be put down, but before any military action could take place against Sheba, David was confronted with the devious nature of his successful general, Joab. Joab had clearly disobeyed David's orders to spare his son Absalom. What Joab did was, without question, the right decision, but as a military man he should not have been permitted to disobey the direct order of his sovereign.

Remember that Amasa, who led the armies of Absalom, was Joab's first cousin. When the status of forces was being agreed upon, Joab learned that it was David's intention to make Amasa head of his army in place of Joab. True to form, Joab arranged a private meeting with Amasa and stabbed him in the stomach, leaving him on the side of the road covered up with a pile of rocks. Joab realized the king, however popular with the people, had no power without the army. Later on, under the reign of Solomon, Joab's life was finally terminated. But until then, despite his arrogance and devious ways, Joab remained in power in the service of King David.

Joab then led the king's armies against the Benjamite rebel, Sheba. So, Joab and his troops were surrounding Sheba's home city when a woman looked down from the wall, and said, "Are you Joab?" Joab replied, "Yes, I am." She further asked, "Who are you seeking?" Joab replied, "I am looking for a rebel named Sheba, son of Bikri, from the hill country of Ephraim. Turn him over to us and we will spare your city."

The wise woman brought Joab's ultimatum to the elders of the city who immediately seized Sheba and cut off his head. The woman then threw Sheba's head over the wall to the feet of Joab, and Joab and the troops withdrew from that city.

With the demise of Sheba and the war having ended with Absalom, David was now in full control of Israel.

However, it seemed that despite David's many victories, the Philistines were still attempting to defeat and subjugate Israel. David once again led the armies of Israel into battle, but we learn that in one battle he became exhausted, and Ishbi-Benob, who was a giant, came close to killing David. But Abishai son of Zeruiah, the mother of Joab, came to David's rescue, struck the Philistine down and killed him. Then the men of Israel said to David, "You cannot any longer go out with us to battle so that the lamp of Israel will not be extinguished." In other words, David became synonymous with God's presence in Israel. His leadership was vital to the nation. His presence united the nation. They could no longer risk losing the light of that country for just one battle against their enemies, the Philistines.

CHAPTER TWENTY-FOUR

David Dances for Joy

Going back now to a point earlier in David's reign, when his new capital was established in Jerusalem, and there was relative prosperity throughout the country, David decided that the time had come to bring the Ark of the Covenant to a new place in the capital city of Jerusalem (2 Samuel 6).

The Ark was placed on a new cart pulled by oxen. Along the way, the oxen stumbled and it appeared that the Ark might fall to the ground. Uzzah, the son of Abinadab, saw the Ark ready to fall and he reached out his hand to steady it. When he touched the Ark, he was struck dead and fell beside the road. Obviously, David thought he was doing a good thing, but this good thing resulted in the death of one of his men. He was perplexed, perhaps angry, but certainly afraid of what would happen next. Rather than proceed further, the cart carrying the Ark was taken to the home of Obed-Edom the Gittite, where it remained for three months, during which time God blessed Obed-Edom's household.

David then learned that rings were on the side of the Ark to accommodate poles, and the poles were to be carried on the shoulders of priests—not on ox carts. So, the appropriate priests were designated to carry the Ark on their shoulders. And this time they entered Jerusalem in a joyous procession.

David was so overjoyed and so much in love with the Lord, that he began to dance wildly. Apparently David had a tunic on, but was wearing no undergarments. So as he danced about, his private parts were on full display to the young girls who were along the side of the road.

Remember that David had married Michal, the younger daughter of King Saul. After the Ark had been settled and David gave some celebratory food to those assembled, he went to his home full of happiness and joy. Surprisingly, he encountered an angry wife who snarled at him, "What kind of a spectacle did the king make today, exposing himself to the young maidens along the way?" David replied, "It was before the Lord that I danced, the same Lord that put me in the kinship in the place of your father. And I will be honored by the young girls that you claim were offended by my conduct."

We are told from that moment on, Michal had no more children. Probably her scorn and disdain for her exuberant husband were enough to assure her a remote place in the harem with no connubial relations for the rest of her life.

CHAPTER TWENTY-FIVE

Promise of a Never-Ending Kingship

After he was settled in his new palace with the Ark of the Covenant now located in a modest building, David decided that he would like to build a magnificent temple to honor the name of Yahweh.

But the Lord sent Nathan the prophet to give David a message (2 Samuel 7). He said that in all the time that Israel had been wandering, God had never asked for a temple to be built in His honor. However, He said to David, "I will build you a house."

> "Now then, tell my servant David, 'This is what the LORD Almighty says: I took you from the pasture, from tending the flock, and appointed you ruler over my people Israel. I have been with you wherever you have gone, and I have cut off all your enemies from before you. Now I will make your name great, like the names of the greatest men on earth. And I will provide a place for my people Israel and will plant them so that they can have a home of their own and no longer be disturbed. Wicked people will not oppress them anymore, as they did at the beginning and have done ever since the time I appointed leaders over my people Israel. I will also give you rest from all your enemies.

"'The LORD declares to you that the LORD himself will establish a house for you: When your days are over and you rest with your ancestors, I will raise up your offspring to succeed you, your own flesh and blood, and I will establish his kingdom. He is the one who will build a house for my Name, and I will establish the throne of his kingdom forever. I will be his father, and he will be my son. When he does wrong, I will punish him with a rod wielded by men, with floggings inflicted by human hands. But my love will never be taken away from him, as I took it away from Saul, whom I removed from before you. Your house and your kingdom will endure forever before me; your throne will be established forever.'" (2 Samuel 7:8–16)

David was overwhelmed by the word that had been given to him. So he sat before the Lord and prayed:

"Who am I, Sovereign LORD, and what is my family, that you have brought me this far? And as if this were not enough in your sight, Sovereign LORD, you have also spoken about the future of the house of your servant—and this decree, Sovereign LORD, is for a mere human!

"What more can David say to you? For you know your servant, Sovereign LORD. For the sake of your word and according to your will, you have done this great thing and made it known to your servant.

"How great you are, Sovereign LORD! There is no one like you, and there is no God but you, as we have heard with our own ears. And who is like your people Israel—the one nation on earth that God went out to redeem as a people for himself, and to make a name for himself, and to perform great and awesome wonders by driving out nations and their gods from before your people, whom you redeemed from Egypt? You have established your people Israel as your very own forever, and you, LORD, have become their God.

"And now, LORD God, keep forever the promise you have made concerning your servant and his house. Do as you promised, so that your name will be great forever. Then people will say, 'The LORD Almighty is God over Israel!' And the house of your servant David will be established in your sight.

"LORD Almighty, God of Israel, you have revealed this to your servant, saying, 'I will build a house for you.' So your servant has found courage to pray this prayer to you. Sovereign LORD, you are God! Your covenant is trustworthy, and you have promised these good things to your servant. Now be pleased to bless the house of your servant, that it may continue forever in your sight; for you, Sovereign LORD, have spoken, and with your blessing the house of your servant will be blessed forever." (2 Samuel 7:18–29)

So, God's promise to His servant was that his kingship would be famous throughout all the world and it would never end. No other promise of this magnitude has ever been made to any human being, and it clearly applied to David's descendant, Jesus of Nazareth, who was repeatedly referred to in the New Testament as the Son of David and who, after His resurrection, lives forever.

CHAPTER TWENTY-SIX

David's Mighty Warriors

It was a hot, dusty day during Israel's summer. Some of the men in the Israelite army were resting in the shade. Some had wounds that had been bandaged. Several of the leaders came to David and said, "Your majesty, you are the leader of our army, but we need men of proven ability to serve as commanders under your leadership."

These leaders had to be men of extraordinary bravery and ability. So, David chose a group of mighty men. Three of the men stood out from the others. Here are their extraordinary accomplishments.

"These are the names of David's mighty warriors:

Josheb-Basshebeth, a Tahkemonite, was chief of the Three; he raised his spear against eight hundred men, whom he killed in one encounter.

Next to him was Eleazar son of Dodai the Ahohite. As one of the three mighty warriors, he was with David when they taunted the Philistines gathered at Pas Dammim for battle. Then the Israelites retreated, but Eleazar stood his ground and struck down the Philistines till his hand grew tired and froze to the sword. The LORD brought about a great victory that day. The troops returned to Eleazar, but only to strip the dead.

Next to him was Shammah son of Agee the Hararite. When the Philistines banded together at a place where there was a field full of lentils, Israel's troops fled from them. But Shammah took his stand in the middle of the field. He defended it and struck the Philistines down, and the LORD brought about a great victory." (2 Samuel 23:8–12)

"Abishai the brother of Joab son of Zeruiah was chief of the Three. He raised his spear against three hundred men, whom he killed, and so he became as famous as the Three. Was he not held in greater honor than the Three? He became their commander, even though he was not included among them.

Benaiah son of Jehoiada, a valiant fighter from Kabzeel, performed great exploits. He struck down Moab's two mightiest warriors. He also went down into a pit on a snowy day and killed a lion. And he struck down a huge Egyptian. Although the Egyptian had a spear in his hand, Benaiah went against him with a club. He snatched the spear from the Egyptian's hand and killed him with his own spear. Such were the exploits of Benaiah son of Jehoiada; he too was as famous as the three mighty warriors. He was held in greater honor than any of the Thirty, but he was not included among the Three. And David put him in charge of his bodyguard." (2 Samuel 23:18-23)

There were also thirty powerful fighters who were included in a bodyguard for King David. Among them was a man known as Uriah the Hittite, who we previously learned was the husband of a woman named Bathsheba. Taken together, this group of thirty-seven extraordinary fighters became the core leadership of David's army. They were fiercely committed to David—to defend him, to fight with him, and to fulfill his wishes.

On one hot day, David made a comment, "Oh, that someone would get me a drink of water from the well near the gate of Bethlehem!" (2 Samuel 23:15). Unfortunately, Bethlehem was now a Philistine stronghold, and for three of David's men to slip into the town to draw water from the well and slip out unnoticed would have been considered a suicide mission. Nevertheless, three of the thirty warriors made such a journey, obtained the water at the risk of their lives, and then reported back to David. He took the water from their hands and said, "You have risked your lives to bring me a drink of water. I can't accept this sacrifice, even if it was done in love for me." So David poured the water out before the Lord rather than drink water that could have caused the death of his brave warriors.

CHAPTER TWENTY-SEVEN

David's Sinful Census

We now turn to a part of David's life which has resulted in theological controversy ever since it was set down in the Bible. In 2 Samuel 24:1, we read these words: "Again the anger of the LORD burned against Israel, and he incited David against them, saying, 'Go and take a census of Israel and Judah.'"

It is certainly hard to understand why, if David was obeying a great command of the Lord, he and his people would in turn be punished because of it. However, in 1 Chronicles 24:1, the narrative makes Satan the author of this instruction and this, of course, makes more sense as we consider it.

Think what a census does. In modern-day America the census reveals how many family units are in a country; the extent of their resources; how many able-bodied men may be available for military draft; and, more recently, how many seats the House of Representatives can be allocated to a particular state because of its population.

Just recently, the census in the United States has shown states like Texas gaining seats, and states like New York and Illinois losing seats. This political makeup was not the case in David's Israel, but what was the case was that only God Himself could order a census.

The census described in the Book of Exodus was to show God's claim over the male children of the people and a tax that they were to pay to be exempt from whatever penalty was to be imposed. We learn also that before the nation of Israel entered the Promised Land, God instructed Moses to take a census of all the people who remained—those roughly age twenty and younger—after their elders had died in the wilderness. This census was clearly for the purpose of allocating enough land so that the more numerous tribes could have enough space to accommodate their needs. Neither of these national censuses was sinful. Of course, all of the people belonged to God and perhaps only God Himself should have ordered a census. Therefore, assuming the idea of a census of Israel either came from Satan or from David's own imagination clearly meant a usurping of God's ownership of the people. Could the census have been a manifestation of ego to determine how big an army was at his disposal, or to determine how much territory he might seek to take away from his neighbors? We have no way of knowing.

However, we do know that, although Joab and all the commanders of the army objected to the census as being dangerous and ungodly, King David's word prevailed against their strong advice. So, Joab and the commanders went throughout the country to perform the count.

While the census was underway, God sent the prophet Gad to David to inform him that He was displeased at what David was doing. The Lord offered him three choices of punishment (1 Chronicles 21:11–15):

> "So Gad went to David and said to him, 'This is what the LORD says: "Take your choice: three years of famine, three months of being swept away before your enemies, with their swords over-taking you, or three days of the sword of the LORD—days of plague in the land, with the angel of the LORD ravaging every part of Israel." Now then, decide how I should answer the one who sent me.'

David said to Gad, 'I am in deep distress. Let me fall into the hands of the LORD, for his mercy is very great; but do not let me fall into human hands.'

So the LORD sent a plague on Israel, and seventy thousand men of Israel fell dead. And God sent an angel to destroy Jerusalem. But as the angel was doing so, the LORD saw it and relented concerning the disaster and said to the angel who was destroying the people, 'Enough! Withdraw your hand.' The angel of the LORD was then standing at the threshing floor of Araunah the Jebusite."

On that day, Gad went to David and said, "Go up and build an altar to the Lord on the threshing floor of Araunah the Jebusite." So, in obedience to this instruction, David climbed up the hill. Araunah saw him coming, and he bowed down before the king. He asked David, "Why are you here?" And David said, "I have come to buy your threshing floor and build an altar to the Lord so that the plague will be stopped." Araunah was delighted at this news and he quickly blurted out, "Here is my threshing sledge. You can use the wood and I will slaughter my oxen that you can use for sacrifice."

David shook his head and made this memorable comment, "No, I insist on paying you for it. I will not sacrifice to the Lord my God burnt offerings that cost me nothing." So, David built the altar, made the sacrifice, and the plague throughout Israel stopped. David bought the threshing floor and the oxen for six hundred shekels of silver, and built an altar to the Lord and sacrificed burnt offerings and fellowship offerings. Then the plague in Israel stopped.

This place has enormous historic significance. It is known as Mount Moriah. It is at this place that not only did Abraham prepare to offer his son, Isaac, as a sacrifice in obedience to the command of the Lord, but where Solomon built the temple to the name of the Lord. It was

also at this place where an eighth-century Christian church was demol-
ished by Muslims and in its place they built the architectural feature
seen prominently in Jerusalem, known as the Dome of the Rock.

Successive waves of conquerors have tried to assert sovereignty over
Jerusalem. The Ottomans, the Turks, and more recently the PLO have
tried to assert sovereignty over this small piece of territory. But whatever their claims may be, the ownership of the Temple Mount clearly
belongs to the descendants of David, who bought it from Araunah for
six hundred shekels of silver. No other modern-day group can assert a
prior claim over that of David himself.

CHAPTER TWENTY-EIGHT

Adonijah's Palace Coup—Solomon Named King

When King David began to move along in age, his battle wounds and incredible physical exertions began to tell in his body. Despite how many blankets he had on, he could not get warm. His advisors said, "Let's search the nation for a beautiful, young virgin who can lie next to the king and keep him warm." This was in a time when glass windows were unknown and other forms of heating material were not considered practical. David's advisors searched throughout Israel for a beautiful girl and found Abishag, a Shunammite, and brought her to the king. Abishag was a very beautiful girl, and she slept with King David, but he had no intimate relations with her.

We learn that Adonijah was quite handsome and was next in the line of King David's sons after Absalom. Adonijah conferred with Joab, who we believe was always self-serving and devious, and with Abiathar the priest to gain their support. It seems that the holy people had their share of palace intrigue, especially when it came to transfer of power. Now Adonijah, whose mother was Haggith, put himself forward and said, "I will be king." So he got fifty men together and chariots to run before him and proclaim that he was to be king.

Nathan the Prophet, Benaiah (David's special guard), along with Zadok the priest did not join Adonijah's palace coup. In those days, it was quite certain that if a coup took place, the rival would be put to death—and this meant that Joab and Adonijah would kill Bathsheba and her son, Solomon, once Adonijah had taken power. So, Nathan quickly hurried to Bathsheba and said, "Are you aware that Adonijah has declared himself king? You must demand that the king affirm his personal choice which was made to you some years ago."

Bathsheba went quickly to King David while Abishag was ministering to him and said, "Are you aware that your son, Adonijah, has declared himself king? You promised me that our son, Solomon, would be your successor. What is your pleasure?"

Then Nathan came in to confirm her report and said, "Has your majesty chosen Adonijah your successor? He is now entertaining his brothers, but the celebration did not include me or Zadok the priest or Benaiah or your son Solomon." Then King David acted swiftly and said, "Call in Bathsheba!" And David took this oath with Bathsheba: "As surely as the LORD lives, who has delivered me out of every trouble, I will surely carry out this very day what I swore to you by the LORD, the God of Israel: Solomon your son shall be king after me, and he will sit on my throne in my place" (1 Kings 1:29–30). Then David said, "Call in Zadok the priest, Nathan the prophet and Benaiah son of Jehoiada." When they came before the king, he said to them: "Take your lord's servants with you and have Solomon my son mount my own mule and take him down to Gihon. There have Zadok the priest and Nathan the prophet anoint him king over Israel. Blow the trumpet and shout, 'Long live King Solomon!'" (vv. 32–34).

At that, Adonijah's coronation party came to an end. His guests realized that the palace coup had failed, and all of them might lose their lives as a result. Adonijah came to Solomon and said, "I am looking for mercy." And Solomon assured him as long as he lived a worthy life, he would be spared.

David was delighted that at the end of a long and productive life he could see his own son succeed him in a peaceful transition of power. However, the record now reveals a side of David that was completely unworthy of a great leader.

You can almost see David placing his arm around his son, Solomon, and saying, "Solomon, there are a few things that I would like for you to do after my death. You remember how Joab murdered Abner and Amasa. He killed them shedding blood in peace time, and that blood stained the belt around his waist. Do not let his gray hair go down to the grave in peace. And remember you have Shimei, the son of Gera, who called down bitter curses on me the day I went to Mahanaim. You are a man of wisdom. You know what to do with him. Bring his gray head down to the grave in blood." Of course, there was one act of kindness. He said, "Remember to show kindness to the sons of Barzillai the Gileadite, and let them be among ones who sit at your table, because they stayed with me when I fled from Absalom" (1 Kings 2).

Then we read David rested with his fathers and was buried in the City of David. He had reigned forty years over Israel—seven years in Hebron, and thirty-three in Jerusalem. So, Solomon sat on the throne of his father, David, and his rule was firmly established.

CHAPTER TWENTY-NINE

A Plan for a Temple and David's Enormous Wealth

The Lord had clearly told David that he, David, was not the one to build the temple because he was a man of war and had shed blood in battle. His son, Solomon, had been chosen by God to build the temple. But actually building it and preparing for its construction were apparently two different things.

David gave precise instructions as to the quantity of gold and silver to be used in various kinds of sacred articles to be used in service. The temple was to contain bowls for incense, lampstands, the table for the consecrated bread, forks, sprinkling bowls, pitchers, and the altar of incense. He also gave Solomon the plan for the "chariot," that is, the cherubim that spread their wings of gold and covered the Ark of the Covenant of the Lord.

"All this," David said, "I have in writing as a result of the LORD's hand on me, and he enabled me to understand all the details of the plan" (1 Chronicles 28:19).

We remember a similar instance when God spoke to Moses to build the tabernacle: "See that you make them according to the pattern shown you on the mountain" (Exodus 25:40). In other words, symbolism of the items in the tabernacle, and later in the temple, were intended in some fashion to reflect the majesty of God's heavenly kingdom.

I can understand exactly what occurred with David. When the time came for a CBN headquarters building to be constructed, professional architects were employed who brought forth seven designs for a building, all of which were, for one reason or another, considered unsuitable.

My wife, Dede, said very knowingly, "Why do we have to build another ugly building?" Of course, God had other plans for us and here's what happened…

One Saturday morning I sat down at the head of my dining room table with a piece of paper, a ruler, and a pen. I had asked the Lord for wisdom after having been forced to turn down the work product of experienced architects. As I sat before the table, the concept came to me very clearly, and I sketched out a building which was in the form of a cross and later proved to be the perfect blending of two large studios, a central control room, and backup offices located in perfect symmetry to one another.

Undoubtedly, there are many other instances in contemporary life where God has given inspiration to people who have struggled with a problem until they arrived at what appeared to be an elegant solution.

King David was open to God's suggestion, and God showed him precisely the details of the construction of the temple, as well as the quantities of precious metal to be used for the many sacred instruments.

What becomes really staggering, however, is the enormous wealth that David possessed and gave to build the temple. The phrase is used, "He was wealthy beyond the dreams of avarice." He said the temple of Yahweh must be "of great magnificence and fame and splendor in the sight of all the nations" (1 Chronicles 22:5). So, in building the temple, David was clearly no piker.

Consider the enormous money that David provided: "With all my resources I have provided for the temple of my God—gold for the gold work, silver for the silver, bronze for the bronze, iron for the iron and wood for the wood, as well as onyx for the settings, turquoise, stones of various colors, and all kinds of fine stone and marble—all of these in large quantities" (1 Chronicles 29:2).

Over and above these quantities, David said, "I now give my personal treasures of gold and silver for the temple of my God, over and above everything I have provided for this holy temple: three thousand talents of gold (gold of Ophir) and seven thousand talents of refined silver, for the overlaying of the walls of the buildings, for the gold work and the silver work, and for all the work to be done by the craftsmen." (1 Chronicles 29:3–5).

Three thousand talents of gold! That translates to one hundred and ten metric tons. If we consider that gold today is $1,800 (plus or minus) an ounce, and there are sixteen ounces in a pound—and 2,204.62 pounds to a metric ton, and that is multiplied by 110 metric tons— consider the enormity of his gift. A metric ton of gold in today's market would be approximately $63,493,056, and 110 tons of gold would be $6,984,236,160!

The weight of silver that he gave was seven thousand talents, which is about 240 metric tons. Considering the price of silver today is about $24 an ounce, 240 metric tons would be approximately $203,177,779. And the weight of other materials given is equally enormous.

Therefore, we can add to David's other accomplishments that he was one of the richest people on the face of the earth circa 1,000 BC.

So, with what had been provided to Solomon, the Lord's temple was indeed a wonder. Exactly what David had hoped—magnificent and of fame throughout all the earth.

Time and again, the Bible describes the temple as a structure built for the "name of the Lord." It was to honor His name and that is abundantly clear. It is easy to fall into a trap of thinking that a temple is the home of the deity. Undoubtedly, many religions believe that the temples they have built, and that often contain a large statue of their deity, somehow contained that deity. But how could any structure on earth contain the Creator of the earth?

Dr. Hugh Ross, an adjunct Professor at Regent University, and a noted astrophysicist, made this statement about the universe: "In the universe there exists one billion trillion stars the size of our sun."

Think of it… One billion trillion stars the size of our sun. Although the earth we inhabit seems uniquely situated in the vast universe as a habitation of individuals made in the image of God, that does not diminish the fact that our planet is part of a relatively small solar system which, in turn, is a part of the Milky Way Galaxy, which, in turn, occupies a small part of what is known as the Spiral Nebulae.

If heaven is God's throne, and the earth is His footstool, how could any of us possibly build a structure worth of such a deity?

So, David was entirely proper in saying the temple that he built, as beautiful as it was, was only to honor the name of "He who causes everything to be."

CHAPTER THIRTY

The Shepherd King Exalts His Shepherd

Perhaps the best-known psalm in history is Psalm 23, in which the shepherd king puts himself in the role of a sheep and Yahweh his Lord becomes the Shepherd. Think of what he said: "He makes me to lie down in green pastures." When David was taking care of his father's sheep, he picked out the luscious green grass and the pastures which were more pleasant for his sheep.

He also says, "You prepare a table before me in the presence of my enemies." Around the sheep that David was tending were wolves and bears and lions, all waiting to devour members of David's flock. However when they were enjoying the rich pasture grass, they were safe because their shepherd was keeping them free from their enemies.

We go on to think that the rocks and hills surrounding Judea were extremely dangerous for the sheep. The shepherd needed a crook to rescue them. "Your rod and Your staff, they comfort me." The staff was used to protect the sheep, to rescue the sheep, to take little sheep away from danger, to set them upright in case their muscles froze and they were unable to stand (or what is known as cast), and to make sure that they were on the right course.

The time came when it was dark and valleys seemed precipitous, yet the sheep knew that as long as their shepherd was guiding them, they did not need to fear the darkness or the valleys. We read in the Bible "the valley of the shadow of death," but a better translation is a valley of deep darkness. Obviously, that deep darkness would be enough to terrify a human being or a sheep. But the sheep under David's control were not afraid of any danger because their shepherd was with them.

Then, of course, he concludes, "Surely goodness and mercy shall follow me all the days of my life; And I will dwell in the house of the Lord forever."

Obviously no sheep would have thoughts like this, so David would impose his own view on this passage. But here for all of us I want to lay out perhaps the greatest of all the psalms. We know that there are seventy-five psalms in the Bible which bear David's name, but the twenty-third is the most famous of all.

Here now are the words of the man who shepherded his nation for many years (Psalm 23 NKJV).

The LORD is my shepherd;

I shall not want.

He makes me to lie down in green pastures;

He leads me beside the still waters.

He restores my soul;

He leads me in the paths of righteousness

For His name's sake.

Yea, though I walk through the valley of the shadow of death,

I will fear no evil;

For You are with me;

Your rod and Your staff, they comfort me.

You prepare a table before me in the presence of my enemies;

You anoint my head with oil;

My cup runs over.

Surely goodness and mercy shall follow me

All the days of my life;

And I will dwell in the house of the LORD

Forever.

CHAPTER THIRTY-ONE

The Impact of David throughout Sacred History

It is amazing to realize how central David was to the thinking of all those who followed him. For example, in the Jewish tradition, the Sabbath became a religious subset. The rabbis had amassed a book of regulations dealing with the Sabbath. There were so many steps or meters a person could walk on a Sabbath day. A Jewish person could not collect a debt on a Sabbath day. They could not cook on the Sabbath. Not only could they not work, they could not practice medicinal healing on the Sabbath, and so it went.

One day, we learned that Jesus and His disciples were walking through a field of grain on the Sabbath. They were reaching down to the heads of grain and rolling them around in their hands and then eating them. Their critics were quick to assert, "You are working on the Sabbath."

Think of what Jesus Christ, who is the Son of God, used to validate what He and His disciples were doing. He said, "Do you not remember how David, when he was fleeing from Saul, was given the Holy Showbread which was unlawful for any but the priests to eat." Then He went on to say that because of what David did, He, Jesus Christ, was Lord of the Sabbath. Just imagine—Jesus, the Son of God, used the act of His ancestor, David, to validate His own action and to declare the meaning of the Sabbath.

Consider also the Apostle Paul, who was explaining to the Romans how justification by faith works. His authority among others became Abraham and David, who was quoted as saying, "Blessed is the man to whom the Lord will not impute iniquity." Again David became the authority.

Paul also quoted one of the psalms which does not bear David's name to indicate a type of curse on people: "Let their table become a snare." Perhaps the Holy Spirit led Paul to take that particular line of the psalm out of context, but nevertheless in order to validate his own statement, he explained to his readers that what he was saying was a quote from King David.

We go back into the time of the kings who succeeded David, and we find Abijah, who was king of Judah, which was at war with the Israelites under Jeroboam. Abijah shouted out, "Don't you know that the LORD, the God of Israel, has given the kingship of Israel to David and his descendants forever by a covenant of salt? . . . And now you plan to resist the kingdom of the LORD, which is in the hands of David's descendants" (2 Chronicles 13:5, 8). In other words, the authority for ruling the kingdom of Judah was to be given by God's promise to David's descendants. Once again, we see the ongoing effect of his remarkable life.

In 2 Chronicles, when the priest Jehoiada was attempting to place on the throne the heir of David, it is said that he made a covenant that he and the people and the king would be the Lord's people. So, "Jehoiada placed the oversight of the temple of the LORD in the hands of the Levitical priests, to whom David had made assignments in the temple, to present the burnt offerings of the LORD as written in the Law of Moses, with rejoicing and singing, as David had ordered" (2 Chronicles 23:18)

In other words, the ritual that was to be observed for hundreds of years was according to the express directions given by David, which in turn were followed by successive kings. His plan for the Levites, his plan for the singers, and his order of worship, were accepted practices for hundreds of years throughout the history of Israel.

Jerusalem was taken by the Babylonians in 586 BC, and before that time, the prophet Jeremiah brought forth a message to the people of Israel looking for a future restoration, even though the city might be taken by the Babylonians and the king taken into exile.

> "The word of the LORD came to Jeremiah: 'This is what the LORD says: "If you can break my covenant with the day and my covenant with the night, so that day and night no longer come at their appointed time, then my covenant with David my servant—and my covenant with the Levites who are priests ministering before me—can be broken and David will no longer have a descendant to reign on his throne.
>
> I will make the descendants of David my servant and the Levites who minister before me as countless as the stars in the sky and as measureless as the sand on the seashore."
>
> The word of the LORD came to Jeremiah: 'Have you not noticed that these people are saying, "The LORD has rejected the two kingdoms he chose"? So they despise my people and no longer regard them as a nation. This is what the LORD says: "If I have not made my covenant with day and night and established the laws of heaven and earth, then I will reject the descendants of Jacob and David my servant and will not choose one of his sons to rule over the descendants of Abraham, Isaac and Jacob. For I will restore their fortunes and have compassion on them."'
> (Jeremiah 33:19–26)

In this amazing statement, God instructs the prophet Jeremiah to bring forth these words: "'The days are coming,' declares the LORD, 'when I will fulfill the good promise I made to the people of Israel and Judah. In those days and at that time I will make a righteous Branch sprout from David's line; he will do what is just and right in the land. In those days Judah will be saved and Jerusalem will live in safety. This is the name by which it will be called: The LORD Our Righteous Savior'" (Jeremiah 33:14–16).

Then Yahweh goes on to say, "David will never fail to have a man to sit on the throne of Israel, nor will the Levitical priests ever fail to have a man to stand before me continually" (Jeremiah 33:17–18).

Speaking through the prophet Jeremiah (before the fall of Jerusalem to Babylon) the God of all the universe makes this incredible promise: "If you can break my covenant with the day and my covenant with the night … then my covenant with David my servant—and my covenant with the Levites who are priests ministering before me—can be broken and David will no longer have a descendant to reign on his throne" (Jeremiah 33:20–21).

Then God makes one more extraordinary promise—that the descendants of David His servant and the Levites who minister before Him will be "as countless as the stars in the sky and as measureless as the sand on the seashore" (Jeremiah 33:22).

Once again, we can only stand in amazement at the special love that God has for His servant, David, and His promises for an everlasting kingship in David's hand. We will see later in this chapter the parallel between Jesus Christ and David, but here in the words of the prophet, as the country is facing potential doom, is a measure of hope for an everlasting kingdom that will be named after David, the Shepherd King.

The prophet Isaiah in the eleventh chapter is thought to be revealing the thousand-year time of God's blessing on earth. But consider who is going to be the leader in this time of blessedness (Isaiah 11:1–3):

> A shoot will come up from the stump of Jesse;
> from his roots a Branch will bear fruit.
> The Spirit of the LORD will rest on him—
> the Spirit of wisdom and of understanding,
> the Spirit of counsel and of might,
> the Spirit of the knowledge and fear of the LORD—
> and he will delight in the fear of the LORD.
> He will not judge by what he sees with his eyes,
> or decide by what he hears with his ears.

Isaiah goes on to say, "In that day the Root of Jesse will stand as a banner for the peoples; the nations will rally to him, and his resting place will be glorious" (Isaiah 11:10).

This quote clearly applies to the Messiah, Jesus of Nazareth. Isaiah's writing regarding the Branch of the stump of Jesse applies initially to David, but later and more fully, to Jesus.

When we turn to the Book of Revelation, there is a description by the Apostle John, who was in the Spirit on the Lord's day. He was approached by Jesus who gave him a charge to the seven churches in Asia. To each of the churches there is a commendation and a criticism. However, there are two churches that have no criticism at all. One of those churches is the church of Philadelphia. Here is what John wrote to the angel of the church in Philadelphia:

> "These are the words of him who is holy and true, who holds the key of David. What he opens no one can shut, and what he shuts no one can open. I know your deeds. See, I have placed before you an open door that no one can shut. I know that you

have little strength, yet you have kept my word and have not denied my name. . . . Since you have kept my command to endure patiently, I will also keep you from the hour of trial that is going to come on the whole world to test the inhabitants of the earth." (Revelation 3:7–8, 10)

It is amazing to the average reader to understand how Jesus and David seem to be juxtaposed over and over again in these parts of the Bible. Obviously Jesus was the Son of David and was called the Son of David repeatedly, and His relationship with David was profound.

Here's another example of David's authority in the Bible. The word *pente* means "fifty," and Pentecost was a feast that took place fifty days after the Passover. Jesus was crucified on Passover weekend, and we are told that the apostles gathered together in an upper room on the Day of Pentecost. Before they began serious praying, there was a bit of housekeeping that was needed.

Judas Iscariot had betrayed Jesus and, in his shame, had committed suicide. So, it was important for the apostles to round out the number by replacing Judas with a man they chose. At this point, Peter spoke to the assembled group with these words, "Brothers, the Scripture had to be fulfilled which the Holy Spirit spoke long ago through the mouth of David concerning Judas" (Acts 1:16). I am once again impressed that the authority to make the decisions, such as choosing the twelfth apostle, would be referred to the authority of David.

Peter then went on to say in Acts 1:20, "It is written in the Book of Psalms: 'May his place be deserted; let there be no one to dwell in it,' and, 'may another take his place of leadership.'" Those two quotes were taken from Psalms 69 and 109. It is highly unlikely that David, when writing these words, was given any insight into Judas Iscariot. Nevertheless, the Apostle Peter affirmed that the Holy Spirit had given

David this insight, and from these two psalms he learned that the office that Judas held would be deserted and another would take his place.

Most scholars would presume that one Scripture should refer in one fashion to another by a logical progression. In this case, the Holy Spirit apparently spoke to Peter to use these two psalms to authenticate the choosing of Matthias as the twelfth apostle. Having given the scriptural foundation for their actions, they then cast lots and appointed Matthias.

I, for one, have always felt that God's choice for the twelfth apostle was Saul of Tarsus. Whatever the case, this is one more example of the impact of David throughout the history of the Christian church.

In addition to that, on the day of Pentecost, when the power of God was manifested, and Peter addressed the crowd that had assembled, he again, wanted to bring up David as the final source of his authority. These are the words that He spoke concerning David.

> "Fellow Israelites, listen to this: Jesus of Nazareth was a man accredited by God to you by miracles, wonders and signs, which God did among you through him, as you yourselves know. This man was handed over to you by God's deliberate plan and foreknowledge; and you, with the help of wicked men, put him to death by nailing him to the cross. But God raised him from the dead, freeing him from the agony of death, because it was impossible for death to keep its hold on him. David said about him:
>
> "'I saw the Lord always before me.
> Because he is at my right hand,
> I will not be shaken.
> Therefore my heart is glad and my tongue rejoices;
> my body also will rest in hope,
> because you will not abandon me to the realm of the dead,

you will not let your holy one see decay.
You have made known to me the paths of life;
you will fill me with joy in your presence.'

"'Fellow Israelites, I can tell you confidently that the patriarch David died and was buried, and his tomb is here to this day. But he was a prophet and knew that God had promised him on oath that he would place one of his descendants on his throne. Seeing what was to come, he spoke of the resurrection of the Messiah, that he was not abandoned to the realm of the dead, nor did his body see decay. God has raised this Jesus to life, and we are all witnesses of it. Exalted to the right hand of God, he has received from the Father the promised Holy Spirit and has poured out what you now see and hear. For David did not ascend to heaven, and yet he said,

"The Lord said to my Lord:
'Sit at my right hand
until I make your enemies
a footstool for your feet.'"

'Therefore let all Israel be assured of this: God has made this Jesus, whom you crucified, both Lord and Messiah.'" (Acts 2:22–36)

Deeper in the Book of Revelation, there is a description of angels who hold scrolls in their hands, and an angel says, "Who is worthy to break the seals and open the scroll?" Yet no one could be found. And John the Revelator says:

"I wept and wept because no one was found who was worthy to open the scroll or look inside. Then one of the elders said to me, 'Do not weep! See, the Lion of the tribe of Judah, the Root of David, has triumphed. He is able to open the scroll and its seven seals.'" (Revelation 5:4–5)

It is Jesus Christ who is capable of opening the sacred scroll, and the description of Him in Revelation is of the Lion of the tribe of Judah, the Root of David.

In the very last chapter of Revelation, Jesus is identified with these words:

"Look, I am coming soon! My reward is with me, and I will give to each person according to what they have done. I am the Alpha and the Omega, the First and the Last, the Beginning and the End. Blessed are those who wash their robes, that they may have the right to the tree of life and may go through the gates into the city." (Revelation 22:12–14)

Then we learn these words: "I, Jesus, have sent my angel to give you this testimony for the churches. I am the Root and the Offspring of David, and the bright Morning Star" (Revelation 22:16).

Can any of us conceive that Jesus Christ, in the last words of the Bible in a profound revelation, identifies Himself as the Root and Offspring of David? Why David? Why not "Son of God"? Why not "conceived by the Holy Spirit"? Why not some other designation? But no... He describes Himself as the Offspring of David, who lived at least a thousand years before Jesus.

It's hard for someone in this twenty-first century to conceive of someone who had such incredible influence that, in the last few words of the Bible, the Son of God identifies Himself as the Offspring of David.

CHAPTER THIRTY-TWO

David's Impact upon Theological Thought

David had no seminary to attend nor, as far as we know, except for his relationship to Samuel, had no mentor to teach him profound theological concepts. Yet he lived out a walk with God which gives a lie to the theological concept of determinism and the bound will. In other words, is our life fixed when we are born? What role does our experience play in our mental development? Is there a God in heaven who set the world in motion and then left it to run according to fixed laws? Is a person's destiny fixed at birth? Are we bound by sin and, therefore, unable to break free on our own, or must we have a supernatural intervention to set us free from sinful tendencies?

Libraries are filled with the musings of theologians who come up with complex solutions or theories to explain God's relation to mankind. In the process, we have in today's world dozens of Christian denominations, not to mention non-Christian cults and belief systems. The term *atheist* means "no god." In other words, people who are atheist do not believe God exists. The term *agnostic* means "not knowing." An agnostic is someone who doesn't know one way or the other. In today's world, millions of people are asked, "Do you believe in God?" If they answer "Yes," one could also reply, "Yes, even the devil believes in God and trembles."

A person's belief system will powerfully affect his or her actions as worked out in day-to-day living. The Greeks and Romans had gods that were created out of their own imagination. These gods were endowed with supernatural powers but also were victims of the same foibles that bedevil human beings. In truth, a person with a false god will find it difficult to rise much higher than the god he or she has created. That's why David's belief in a supernatural God who has all wisdom and is completely loving should be the standard for all of us.

Consider for a moment the beautiful minuet that was played out between David and Yahweh, and which is recorded in 1 Samuel 23. David was told, "Look, the Philistines are fighting against Keilah and are looting the threshing floors."

David inquired of Yahweh saying, "Shall I go and attack these Philistines?" Here again is not some impersonal deity, but one who is in direct contact with His servant. People make a great deal of believing that no individual is able to have a "pipeline" to God. Yet David inquired of the Lord and said to Him, "Shall I go and attack these Philistines?"

The Lord answered him, "Go, attack the Philistines and save Keilah."

But David's men hadn't heard this instruction and said, "If we go to Keilah, we will be destroyed." Then we learn that once more, David inquired of Yahweh, and Yahweh answered him.

We take so much for granted and we believe so little. God wants to talk to His people. In the Garden of Eden we are told Adam walked with God in the cool of the evening. The Creator of this universe desires to talk to people, yet there are so many who disagree with this or think there is a fixed decree that events will happen regardless of human activity. How does the concept of predestination and foreknowledge comport with the concept of free will? The Apostle Paul described it very clearly when he advised his followers to "work out their own salvation with fear and trembling, for it is God who works in you to do both His will and His good pleasure."

Paul's advice mirrors David's experience. David is asking. God is directing. The outcome seems a result of joint communications between God Almighty and His servant. The Lord said to David, "Go down to Keilah, for I am going to give the Philistines into your hand." So, David and his men went to Keilah, fought the Philistines, and carried off their livestock. He inflicted heavy losses and saved the people of Keilah. This was standard procedure for David all his life. He asked of God, and God answered him. He gained success because he was God's servant.

We learn something else from David which is instructive for us today. David did not hesitate to place his own relatives in charge of his forces. His generals were his nephews. He was not worried about the charge of nepotism which we hear today. In truth, some of the best-run corporations in America are family businesses. Think of the DuPont family, think of Johnson and Johnson, think of the Ford family, and dozens of others. Yet in today's world there is a presumption that family members will collude against the best interests of stockholders, and only "independent directors" are able to give the advice that's necessary to avoid some kind of corruption. David didn't see it that way.

Something else about David is that he hired on the basis of merit. His mighty men were those who exhibited extraordinary skill in battle. He picked the best for his troops. There were the three, then the thirty, then the Palace Guards. All were highly skilled and proven warriors. He could have given excellent advice to the political leaders of the United States who are insisting on racial or sexual diversity in hiring and who have actually passed laws which legislate against companies that make decisions in their hiring practices based on merit and ability rather than on some theoretical concept of diversity.

CHAPTER THIRTY-THREE

David versus Darwin

When David was under the stars thinking about God and the majesty of God's creation, he asked two questions—what is man, and why do You care for him? The answer is very revealing. "<u>You made</u> him a little lower than the angels," and "<u>You made</u> him ruler over the works of your hands" (Psalm 8:5, 6).

Without question, David's theology conceived of a human being that was made by Yahweh. This human being was established in the order of things just a little lower than the angelic beings, and was given dominion over everything that had been made on the earth. To David, the human being was a unique creation of God Almighty.

In the Genesis account of man's creation by God, he was made *in God's image* (Genesis 1:27). This means that human beings have an ability that no animal possesses—an animal can react to circumstances around him; an animal can show extraordinary creativity in building a nest; an animal can return to an ancient or hereditary birthing place; an animal can fight to protect his own and to obtain his food. However, an animal is not able to commune with a supernatural being nor is he able to mold his environment in any type of profound way. Only man, made in the image of God, can shape his environment in the ways that we have seen the environment change over the centuries of human civilization.

However, in the Darwinians' theory, human beings ascended over millennia of time from tiny, single-cell creatures like the paramecium or the amoeba, which changed into tadpoles and fish in the ocean, and somehow managed to leave the ocean to gain access to dry ground, then adapted their fish scales to become feathers, which in turn became birds, etc.

In fairness, we must state that animals within a particular species do adapt. Animals who don't use their eyes over many years may pass blindness on to their offspring. The same is true with hearing. Russian animal breeders have gone a long way in transforming the character istics of foxes and wolves. We all are familiar with selective breeding to bring out desired characteristics in animals. Luther Burbank made enormous strides in changing the characteristics of various plants.

All of this is clearly true and observable. That does not, however, prove an evolutionary ladder that shows the "descent of man." Although within species, there can clearly be mutations because of environmental challenges or other needs, yet, to posit an overall theorem that will require a transition of up to one million species becomes a bridge too far. We have read of so-called "missing links." Of the estimated one million required to justify Darwinian thought, the million are still "missing."

Here is my personal, rather simplistic view of the fruit of selective breeding.

As a teenager, I worked on a relative's farm. I drove a team of very hardy animals called mules. One was male, the other was female. Their names were Mike and Fly. These mules were the result of a mating between a female horse and a male donkey. Their hardiness was unsurpassed. They could work in the blazing sun all day long and still have boundless energy.

The thing about Mike and Fly that is interesting, however, is that they were both sterile. They were incapable of passing on their excellent qualities to another generation. In other words, to a simple farm boy, it is obvious that the attributes of a common farm animal like a mule cannot be passed on to another generation—or for that matter, added to an evolutionary gene pool.

When the human genome was being explored and discussions centered around DNA, I looked in a volume of the *Encyclopedia Britannica* for information about DNA. I was amazed to read these words, "The DNA produced by evolution for one human being would require a library of one-thousand volumes of five-hundred pages each with single-spaced lines."

I read that and then asked myself, "How could an intelligent person think that 'evolution,' like some mysterious force, wrote out one thousand complicated volumes?" Again, it boggles the imagination to believe that so-called learned people, in an attempt to deny their own privilege as a son or daughter of an all-powerful God, would resort to such clearly fantastic intellectual exercises.

So, again, what is the answer to the question, "What is man?" He or she is a creature made in the image of God somewhat lower than the angels and given dominion over all of God's earthly creation.

The next question that David asked is, "Why are You mindful of man?" I have often asked that question myself. As I am praying, I realize that I inhabit a small planet in the midst of a relatively small solar system in the midst of a small galaxy, and I am one of approximately seven billion people. So, why would an all-powerful God want to listen to me or hear my prayers?

My only assurance in answering that question is the clear message in the Bible that God loves me. This indeed was the profound feeling of David.

One of the most renowned Protestant theologians of the twentieth century was Karl Barth. A student once asked Barth what was the most profound message that he had obtained during years of studies. Barth thought for a moment and said, "Yes, here's what I have learned. Jesus loves me, this I know, because the Bible tells me so."

David's view of mankind was not always benign. When he considered his own transgression in relation to Bathsheba, he wrote these words found in Psalm 51:5: "Surely I was sinful at birth, sinful from the time my mother conceived me."

David also wrote in Psalm 14:2–3: "The Lord looks down from heaven on all mankind to see if there are any who understand, any who seek God. All have turned away, all have become corrupt; there is no one who does good, not even one."

With that gloomy outlook, a person is justified in asking, "What is the way out?" David points out in Psalm 51 that his sin, however heinous it may have been in human terms, was actually against God Himself. And so he cried out to God (vv. 10–11 KJV): "Create in me a clean heart, O God; and renew a right spirit within me. Cast me not away from thy presence; and take not thy holy spirit from me."

There is abundant forgiveness for people who are sincerely repentant for what they have done. David makes clear that a person is not going to overcome the effects of a sinful act on his own. He calls on God to "create in me a clean heart and renew a right spirit within me." He then asks God to "restore the joy of my salvation" and "take not Your Holy Spirit from me." So, there is much debate in today's world among Christians on the topic of "once saved, always saved," or whether it is possible to lose one's salvation. What action would it take to make this happen?

David makes it clear that adultery and murder were heinous sins. When sin of that nature takes place, the joy of God is lifted from a believer's heart. The Bible makes clear that "if I had cherished sin in my heart, the Lord would not have listened" (Psalm 66:18). And that "whoever conceals their sins does not prosper, but the one who confesses and renounces them finds mercy" (Proverbs 28:13).

The best advice anyone can receive in this matter is to keep short accounts with God. Don't let sin and resentment build up in your heart. Don't harbor a grudge in relation to your spouse. Don't let the sun go down on your wrath. David's words and the biblical text make it abundantly clear that we are sinful creatures who have a loving, forgiving God.

We read in the New Testament that the Lord wants "all men to be saved, and to come unto the knowledge of the truth" (1 Timothy 2:4 KJV). But if we deliberately break His commandments and harbor hatred toward others, we will be deprived of the joy which leads to a productive life.

We are told in the New Testament that the loving God is not interested in His people engaging in self-flagellation, but that they might give Him effective service during their lifetime.

We should also remember the words of Jesus Christ who gave a clear description in the Gospel of Mark as to the path one of His followers should take to obtain the miraculous prayer life which can move mountains: "And whenever you stand praying, if you have anything against anyone, forgive him, that your Father in heaven may also forgive you your trespasses" (Mark 11:25 NKJV). Because being forgiven is the prerequisite for miracle-working prayer.

CHAPTER THIRTY-FOUR

A Little Lower than the Angels

David spoke of human beings as being "a little lower than the angels." We can ask ourselves how David, living in Israel in the year 1,000 BC, learned about angels as he obviously refers to them. We might wonder if, during those starry nights when he was tending his sheep, he received angelic visitors. We don't have any specific record of such an account, but nevertheless he was aware of their ranking among God's created beings. And at least before his descendant Jesus Christ entered history, human beings were "a little lower than the angels."

There are many accurate biblical descriptions of angelic beings, but they are not as some artists would make them appear or as some Christians believe to be their function.

In the Book of Exodus, we learn that an "angel of death" descended on the land of Egypt and killed the firstborn of every household in Egypt (Exodus 12:23). But when he saw the blood of the Passover lamb on the lintels and doorposts of the Israelite's houses, he "passed over them" and they were safe from harm, even though death stalked the family of every Egyptian, including that of Pharaoh.

We are also told that God told Moses that He would send His angel to His people to be with them in the Promised Land. And Moses replied to the Lord, "If you don't personally go with us, don't make us leave this place" (Exodus 33:15 NLT).

When Joshua was preparing to cross the Jordan and attack Jericho, a mighty warrior stood before him and Joshua inquired if he was for Israel or for their enemies. And the angel replied, "As Commander of the army of the LORD I have now come" (Joshua 5:14 NKJV).

These enormously powerful beings were so strong that during a siege in Jerusalem by the Assyrian army during the reign of King Hezekiah, one angel went forth and in one night killed 185,000 of the Assyrian troops.

In the Book of Daniel, we learn of an angelic being who stood before Daniel. Here is his description: "I looked up and there before me was a man dressed in linen, with a belt of fine gold from Uphaz around his waist. His body was like topaz, his face like lightning, his eyes like flaming torches, his arms and legs like the gleam of burnished bronze, and his voice like the sound of a multitude" (Daniel 10:5–6). Daniel records, "So I was left alone, gazing at this great vision; I had no strength left, my face turned deathly pale and I was helpless. . . . I fell into a deep sleep, my face to the ground" (Daniel 10:8–9). Then after Daniel was strengthened, the angel said, "Do you know why I have come to you? Soon I will return to fight against the prince of Persia, and when I go, the prince of Greece will come; but first I will tell you what is written in the Book of Truth. (No one supports me against them except Michael, your prince.)" (Daniel 10:20–21). Daniel clearly indicates that there are spiritual beings who control entire nations— some are angelic, some are demonic.

In the New Testament (Matthew 18:10), Jesus said, referring to innocent little children, "Their angels in heaven always see the face of my Father in heaven."

In the Book of Hebrews (Hebrews 1:14), the question is placed, "Are not all angels ministering spirits sent to serve those who will inherit salvation?"

Speaking of His second coming, Jesus says that He will "send his angels with a loud trumpet call, and they will gather his elect from the four winds, from one end of the heavens to the other" (Matthew 24:31).

In the description of the death of Lazarus and the rich man, Jesus said that Lazarus was carried by the angels into Abraham's bosom (Luke 16:22).

When Jesus was being tempted in the wilderness, the devil quoted to Him Psalm 91, which says, "For he will command his angels concerning you to guard you in all your ways" (Psalm 91:11).

When Jesus was praying in the Garden of Gethsemane (Matthew 26) and asking His Father to take the cup of suffering from Him, He told His disciples that He could ask and His Father would send ten legions of angels to assist Him. Ten legions of angels would be enough to destroy the entire nation of Israel, and yet Jesus did not ask for such help because He knew His destiny was to defeat Satan by dying as a representative of all mankind.

In one more reference (1 Corinthians 6:1–3), the Apostle Paul says, "If any of you has a dispute with another, do you dare to take it before the ungodly for judgment instead of before the Lord's people? Or do you not know that the Lord's people will judge the world? And if you are to judge the world, are you not competent to judge trivial cases? Do you not know that we will judge angels? How much more the things of this life!"

I do not believe that the Bible says that each Christian has a special "guardian angel." The angels are here to look after the heirs of salvation, but I am hard-pressed to find any example that says each Christian has a special guardian angel.

I am also tremendously offended by Renaissance art that portrays little children, so-called Putti, as angelic beings. The cherubs, or *cherubim* in Hebrew, were powerful angels whose tasks were to cover the very holiness of God. To equate little babies having wings with such powerful beings is, frankly, an affront.

We do know from the description in Revelation that when the devil, or Lucifer, rebelled against God in heaven, he took a third of the angels with him (Revelation 12:4). These angels became demonic and we are told that the lake of fire in hell is prepared for the devil and his angels (Matthew 25:41).

As a personal aside, years ago when the television team at the Christian Broadcasting Network prepared to enter a new territory for one of our telethons, we prayed to bind the controlling spirits over the particular region where we would be operating. Our prayer was, "Oh God, send the angels." Without question, those faithful messengers went forth and prepared the way, so that when we arrived, we were not engaged in terrible spiritual warfare, but could get on with the task at hand.

CHAPTER THIRTY-FIVE

David and the Big Bang Theory

In Psalm 8, David writes these words: "When I consider your heavens, the work of your fingers, the moon and the stars, which you have set in place" (Psalm 8:3). In reading that, one might ask "why moon and stars?" There is a song with the line "the sun, moon, and stars," but in this psalm, David does not mention the sun. Why not? There is one simple explanation and one that is much more profound.

The simple explanation is easy. David is out under a starry sky at night, and the sun is not shining. Therefore, he does not mention the sun. But on a more profound level, the sun is actually one of the stars. The moon is a subset of the planet earth, so it would be technically incorrect to link the moon and the sun together.

But there is a more profound understanding of this psalm. David affirms that the Lord (Yahweh) set the celestial heaven in place. This comports easily with the meaning of God's name, Yahweh, which means, as we have pointed out earlier in this volume, "He who causes everything to be."

There have been many false claims made about the world in which we live. In the Middle Ages, the average person and scholars believed that the world was flat. They also believed there was a dropping-off point someplace beyond the oceans that would result from a flat earth. It took the voyages of men like Columbus and Magellan to disprove this theory.

In 1608, a Dutchman named Hans Lippershey invented a magnifying device which enabled astronomers to gain a better view of the stars. To such observers was added the voice of an Italian named Galileo who observed that the sun did not revolve around the earth, but that the sun was the center of the solar system, and not earth. For this thought, Galileo was threatened with excommunication by the Catholic Church.

In truth, despite claims of infallibility, the pope was wrong on his understanding of cosmogony. Later on, of course, modern-day scholars have available to them the giant reflecting telescope on Palomar Mountain in California. More recently, they have the Hubble Telescope which was launched into space; free of the earth's atmosphere, it can observe the heavenly bodies with great precision. For several centuries after the perfecting of the telescope, astrophysicists put forth a number of hypothetical cases for the origin of the universe. As a matter of fact, a total of ten so-called cosmogonies were offered by scientists and, over time, were all rejected.

Today, scientists, who have at their disposal incredibly precise measurements, have arrived at a theory which is known as, for want of a better term, the Big Bang Theory. Under this hypothesis, scientists have concluded that approximately five billion years ago, the gases in the known universe were compressed to an unbelievable density at which they exploded and sent forth flaming debris, which cooled to become the galaxies, stars, and planets that we see today.

The question that scientists have to ask is: who or what force caused this incredible compression which, in turn, brought forth our universe? To those of us who are believers, only an all-powerful Creator could have brought this into being.

An Israeli astrophysicist brought this incredible fact to my attention: The force of the "big bang" launched an expanding universe. However, if the amount of matter involved in this process was too little, the universe would fly apart. If the matter was too much, the universe would collapse back on itself and explode. According to this expert, the amount involved was so small that it could be described as ten to the twenty-third power (100,000,000,000,000,000,000,000) of an inch! Consider this incredible precision: one tiny molecule made the difference between the universe that we now enjoy versus one that would have destroyed Itself.

More and more physicists are now saying that because of these extraordinary facts, the universe is tuned for life.

If the universe had evolved from chaos, there would have been no earth, no humanity, no salvation, and no redemption. To David, it was all the work of the "fingers of Yahweh."

Against that setting, we should consider this remarkable planet that we are privileged to inhabit. We live on a planet that has precisely the correct distance from our sun. If we were a bit closer, we would have been burned up in scorching heat. If we were a bit farther away, we would have frozen to death. If the earth was a bit smaller, there would not be adequate gravity for human or animal life to survive. If the earth had been just a bit bigger, human beings and animals would be unable to move. Every step would be an ordeal to fight against gravity. The earth is exactly the right size to maintain an appropriate atmosphere—a bit smaller, and we could not have the air we breathe.

There are many pieces of debris in space. Gravitation can pull them into a collision with a planet; however, our earth has relatively near it a big brother planet named Jupiter, which can attract debris that might otherwise collide with earth.

Our earth has been given a molten core which can set up for us an appropriate magnetic field not only for use by human instruments, but also to protect the earth from isolated radiation.

It is believed that in the formative ages, a planet the size of Mars collided with the yet-unformed Earth and a portion of our planet flew into space to become our moon. The moon has just enough gravitational pull to keep the Earth from spinning wildly like a top.

It is believed that an ice-filled comet crashed into our planet in its early days and filled our oceans with the water that makes us appear from space as the "blue planet."

The incredible details which enable us to enjoy this world have been provided by a loving Father whose wisdom exceeds anything of which we, as humans, can possibly conceive, and we can say with David, "How excellent is thy name in all the earth!" (Psalm 8:1 KJV).

But for us today, when we realize the unbelievable love of our Father for us, and realize what pains were taken over 5 billion years to put in the vastness of the created world a fit habitation for those who were created in the image of God, we can only know that one day we can join the chorus of the angels who sing praises to an all-loving and all-wise deity who, over a span of 5 billion years, brought forth a Son who on this very planet would show forth God's love for this creation, and would demonstrate to principalities and powers that love would triumph and that an all-wise and all-loving God could be trusted to bring forth in the days to come "new heavens and a new earth, wherein dwelleth righteousness" (2 Peter 3:13 KJV).

APPENDIX

Date of first civilization in Sumer: circa 4,500–4,000 BC

Abram leaves Ur: circa 2,000 BC

Abram leaves his family and enters the Promised Land: circa 1,950 BC

Jacob and family enter Egypt: circa 1,875–1,790 BC

Date of Exodus from Egypt: circa 1,375 BC

Dates of David's kingship: circa 1,010–970 BC

Birth of Jesus: circa 4–6 BC

Date of Jesus' crucifixion: circa 30–36 AD

Beginning of Christian church: Day of Pentecost, fifty days after crucifixion, circa 30–36 AD

Pat Robertson is a renowned religious leader, a philanthropist, an educator, and an author. He founded the Christian Broadcasting Network, of which he is chairman, and hosted its flagship program, *The 700 Club*. He is the founder and chancellor of Regent University, the founder of the humanitarian organization Operation Blessing International, and founder of the American Center for Law and Justice.

Born March 22, 1930, Pat graduated magna cum laude with a Bachelor of Arts from Washington and Lee University, earned a Juris Doctor from Yale Law School, and received a master of divinity from New York Theological Seminary.

His twenty-three books include *The Secret Kingdom*, which was the number-one religious book in America.

Pat was married sixty-seven years before his wife, Dede, went home to be with the LORD in 2022. Together, they had four children, fourteen grandchildren, and twenty-three great-grandchildren.

Made in the USA
Columbia, SC
15 June 2023

d3a0ed94-5e8a-4c92-9b4d-969108e87d1fR01